The Waiting Child

How the Faith and Love of One
Orphan Saved the Life of Another

www.stmartins.com

"The Waiting Child" by Debbie Bodie. Copyright © 1997. Reprinted with permission.

Library of Congress Cataloging-in-Publication Data

Champnella, Cindy.
    The waiting child : how the faith and love of one orphan saved the life of another / Cindy Champnella.—1st ed.
        p. cm.
    ISBN 0-312-30963-5 (hc)
    ISBN 0-312-30964-3 (pbk)
    EAN 978-0312-30964-0
    1. Champnella, Jaclyn. 2. Chinese American children—Biography.
3. Adopted children—United States—Biography. 4. Orphans—China—Biography. 5. China—Biography. 6. Intercountry adoption—China. 7. Intercountry adoption—United States. 8. Champnella, Cindy. 9. Adoptive parents—United States—Biography. I. Title.

E184.C5 C443 2003
305.9'06945—dc21
[B]

                                                                2002035759

10 9 8 7 6 5 4 3 2

Praise for *The Waiting Child*

"Sensitively pitched, moving, and refreshingly unsentimental."

—*Kirkus Reviews*

"Jaclyn Champnella's remarkable experiences far exceed a simple love story."

—*The Oakland Press*

"An angel is someone of purity and strength who provides comfort and protection to others . . . (Jaclyn) may be one of the youngest angels, but she is clearly one of the most dedicated and loving."

—Senator Debbie Stabenow, at the 2003 Congressional Coalition "Angel in Adoption" award presentation

"If this story doesn't make your heart ache, you should see a cardiologist. Four-year-old Jaclyn's extraordinary devotion and determination are a powerful lesson in the meaning of love."

—Jill Smolowe, author of *An Empty Lap: One Couple's Journey to Parenthood*

"A riveting tale of adoption that paints a picture of life in a Chinese orphanage and of older children in their new families. While this is Jaclyn's story, it is also much more."

—Lois Gilman, author of *The Adoption Resource Book*

"It is a story about her defying the odds. . . . And, stripped to its core, it is a story about the remarkable making of a family."

—*Detroit News*

"What an amazing story! This is a warm-fuzzy, feel good, uplifting, life- changing story that brings the whole world into perspective."

—*Adoption Today* magazine

"Many adoptive parents can tell amazing tales about how their children joined their family, but few are as remarkable as Cindy and Rick Champnella's."

—*Child Magazine*

"Heartbreaking, searing, painful, but ultimately healing and hopeful."

—Cindy Gallaher, founder and president of North Bay Adoptions and adoptive parent

Cindy Champnella

St. Martin's Griffin ♔ New York

For Jaclyn

My light
My love
My sorrow
My joy

My child

With eternal thanks for bringing your baby to us.

And for the millions of children on this earth like her.
For those who live each day in the never-ending darkness
of a life without a mama
to shield you from the storms,
to hold you when you hurt,
to dry your tears,
to love you. . . .

May you survive, as she did, with your soul intact.
May you hang on to hope, as she did, with both hands.

May you believe.

Contents

Acknowledgments

I feel foolish writing these acknowledgments, because by doing so I'm somehow saying that this is my book, and I knew, I always knew, that this book was never really mine. I was only the conduit—this story has always been Jaclyn's. I know now that God does have a purpose for each of us, even though I had long ago lost sight of that by the time I met Jaclyn. I guess by admitting that, I've made the biggest acknowledgment of all—had it been solely up to me, this book would never have come to fruition.

I need to start by acknowledging my hero, Snow Wu, and her amazing assistant, Andrea Venkat. If it were not for the extraordinary efforts of these two women, I would never have known either Jaclyn or Lee. My special thanks to George and Ginger Keller, the angels who whispered in Snow's ear the story of Jaclyn's heartache. I'm grateful that Snow then offered her help once more—after all she had done to bring Jaclyn here, I could not have asked her for another miracle.

I'm indebted to my circle of family and friends, who watched this story unfold and told me over and over that it had to be shared. I need to especially acknowledge my father and Deb Morse, who supported me at every step and took hours of time to edit my scribbling, and Shari Black, who finally asked me if I understood yet that I was born to be a writer.

I need to also thank those I've never met who wrote and told me how much this story had impacted their lives and urged me to tell it. And I am incredibly moved by the many who have told me that Jaclyn's story has inspired them to pursue an older child adoption. My dream is that this book will add to those numbers.

I still can hardly believe that I was somehow led to an agent of the caliber of Natasha Kern. Not only did she believe in this story, she was willing to put in the time and effort required to work with a first-time writer. And when I got discouraged, when I believed it would never be published, I'll never forget the words that set me right again:

"How can *you* be Jaclyn's mom? Jaclyn never, ever gave up hope." Thanks, Natasha, for making me believe.

I thankfully acknowledge the passion that my editor, Diane Higgins, brought to this project. I am especially grateful that she understood how important the underlying message of faith is in this story and did not want to change that. And to Nichole Argyres, who cheerfully, wonderfully handled all the details involved in making this book come alive, my thanks.

I am deeply appreciative of Debbie Bodie's generosity in allowing me to include her poem—it bolstered my spirits so many times during the long wait to bring Jaclyn home. I hope it will touch others in the same way that it affected me.

My thanks to Kate and Christy for opening their hearts and lives to Jaclyn, and for their patience as she struggled to understand what it really meant to be a sister. I'm convinced that any other siblings would have decked her by now.

My heartfelt thanks, too, to my husband, Rick, who has always believed in me. When he is by my side, I feel like I can do anything.

And finally, first, last and always, my thanks to Jaclyn and Lee for allowing me the honor of telling their story.

The Waiting Child

—Debbie Bodie

I saw you meet your child today
You kissed your baby joyfully
And as you walked away with her
I played pretend you'd chosen me.

I'm happy for the baby, yet
Inside I'm aching miserably
I want to plead as you go by
"Does no one want a child of three?"

I saw you meet your child today
In love with her before you met
And as I watched you take her out
I knew it wasn't my turn yet.

I recognize you from last year!
I knew I'd seen your face before!
But you came for a second babe.
Does no one want a child of four?

I saw you meet your child today
But this time there was something new
A nurse came in and took MY hand
And then she gave my hand to you.

Can this be true? I'm almost six!
And there are infants here you see?
And then you kissed me and I knew
The child you chose this time was me.

Preface

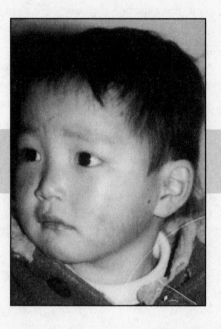

I prayed for this child, and the Lord has granted me what I asked of him.
—I Samuel 1:27

My husband and I began our first Chinese adoption in the summer of 1996. Shortly after our adoption petition was filed with the Chinese government, the adoption process there went through a reorganization, and potential adoptive parents temporarily met a thick wall of silence. No files were processed as the bureaucracy reviewed its systems. Children who desperately needed homes waited. Parents who desperately wanted these children waited, too. I was one of them.

Once the decision to adopt was made, I was anxious to get on with it. I wanted my daughter home. I wanted my daughter home now. Finally, after months without any word, in desperation I made an appointment with a psychic. My faith told me that this was sacrilege. My reason told me that it was foolish. My common sense told me that it was meaningless. But fear had become my constant companion. I feared that we would never hear from China. I feared much more what would happen after we did. Would my comfortable life be forever turned upside down? Would I be up to the challenges this child might bring to us? Fear drove me toward this lunacy as I desperately hoped against hope for some vision of the future.

I sat at the table with the young woman, desperate to believe that she could see my future child, furiously trying to swallow the conviction that she could not, so as not to interfere with the mystical process.

"A boy about three years old," she said firmly. "I see a three-year-old boy in your family's future."

"*What?*" I responded incredulously. Hoping to set her back on the right course, I offered, "We're adopting from China. Virtually all the children available for adoption there are girls." My research had shown me that since the one-child-per-family policy went into effect in the late 1970s, cultural norms dictated a strong preference for boys. Of the literally hundreds of thousands of babies abandoned each year, very few were boys.

She shuffled a few cards, but said again, this time with more emphasis, "I see a three-year-old-boy in your family's future. He will be connected in an unusual way to the girl that you adopt. He will be like a brother, but not a brother."

My skepticism grew, and my pointed glance dismissed her. I left more than a little annoyed at myself. I knew better than to believe in any of this psychic stuff; I took it as another sign of how desperate I had become.

Several months later I received the referral of a four-month-old baby girl and scoffed again at the psychic's prediction. Not until some time later would her words come back to me with a start. And I could not have begun to understand then the journey that would unite me with this special boy.

My first trip to China to adopt my baby, Christy, held no foreboding as to what was to transpire later. My husband, Rick, already had three children from his first marriage. We had a biological daughter, Kate, together. I was certain then that Christy would be our fifth and final child. I would never have believed when I made that journey in January of 1998 that we would make the decision to return to China for another daughter, Jaclyn, after only a few months at home.

Every word you are about to read is true. Even though others might see certain events differently, this is Jaclyn's story from the perspective of the person who knows her best. Names, other than those of my family, have been altered to protect the privacy of those connected to our story. I need to also say this: I love China and am a tireless advocate for Chinese adoption. But I recognize and accept that in this country that I love, many things are done differently than I would do them. I know that I see things through the rose-colored glasses of my Western values. Above all else I need for it to be understood that nothing in this book is meant to criticize or embarrass anyone in China connected with this important process. I know in my heart that the people in China love these children and work tirelessly on their behalf; I have witnessed that love and dedication with my own eyes.

But Jaclyn's eyes have also seen things that I cannot deny. Some have asked me how I could believe the word of one so young. My answer is this: from the beginning she recalled things with too much detail and too much emotion for them to be anything but the truth. Early on, as her story emerged, I was able to contact a woman, who has asked for anonymity, who worked as a volunteer at Jaclyn's orphanage for several years. She has verified what Jaclyn told me. She has also verified what I have seen: conditions that dramatically improve each year, largely due to the donations made by adoptive families.

I need to make this disclaimer: Some parents who have adopted children from this same orphanage say that their children's recall is different. I accept that. I know that children, like adults, can experience the same things and be affected differently by them. What one child remembers as painful, another forgets. But I have also received dozens of private letters from families whose children have related similar things to what Jaclyn has described and, in many cases, much worse, too.

This book is meant to encourage adoptive families and those interested in older child adoption. I have tried to balance this motive with the need to tell Jaclyn's story without whitewashing it. It must be her truth to tell. For this reason, the names of all orphanages, people, and provinces in China are fictitious.

As I got to know Jaclyn, as the events of her past unfurled, the words flowed out of me. I could not hold them in; not to write her story would have been impossible. Through sheer desperation and my need for prayer and support, I began to share her story with others. Almost overnight a network grew of those who prayed not only for both of us but for "Jaclyn's baby" still trapped in China.

For me, the turning point was an incident involving a woman who was very ill with advanced cancer. A friend of hers had compiled all the stories I had written about Jaclyn over the past year and made them into a book for her. She took them with her to read as she endured her chemotherapy treatments. She wrote me a heartfelt letter, which read in part, "I am having a very difficult time with my cancer treatments. But when I get discouraged, when I lose hope, I think of Jaclyn. When I think of how incredibly brave she is, and all that she suffered at the young age that she is, it makes me ashamed of my own fear. When I think of how hopeful she was, even in the dark place where she had been, it makes me realize that I, too, must not lose hope."

It was then that I realized that Jaclyn had a powerful story to tell. She needs me to write it for her, but it is not my story at all. It is a story of pain and suffering and almost unbearable grief. But it is also a story of love and hope and joy and a faith that could move proverbial mountains . . . the faith of a child.

In May of 1999, I got the news that I had waited so long for—Lou Jiao, a four-year-old Chinese orphan whom I had come to love simply from seeing her picture posted for so long on a "waiting children's" list—was to be my new daughter. I thought I knew something of who she was from the history I had been given about her. Filled with emotion over what lay ahead, I poured my heart out in a letter that I put away for her to see when she was older. But when I sat down to write this letter to her, I couldn't have begun to understand the truth of her story.

And so I began what would prove to be the most difficult, but also the most affirming relationship in my life, with this letter to my soon-to-be daughter:

Dear Lou Jiao,

Soon, very soon now, I will be coming to you and asking you to take my hand and leave your whole life behind you. Don't think for a minute that I don't understand how difficult this will be for you. You don't know anything about me. Not what I look like, or who I am, or where I am taking you. You are being asked to trust in a world that has already betrayed your trust. You are being asked to hold on to someone again when the losses you have already borne of those you loved would stagger most adults. You are being asked to make me your mother when you surely have a memory of the other woman you called mother. How strange and confusing this must all seem to you. I hope you will be able to look beyond the blond hair that will be so unfamiliar to you, the face so different from any you have known, into my eyes, which are a color you may never have seen. Look beyond the tears that will certainly be there and search them for my love for you. Then take my hand.

It seems unfair that you do not have any say in all this. And as difficult as the long wait has been for me, I can only imagine how it has seemed to you. I can only imagine the eternity that each day must seem like when you live in a place with no lights, no heat, and no family. Twice you have been told that a family is coming to adopt you. Twice you have been left behind. You have been the victim too long of a system in which children have no voice.

I am bringing with me a big bear of a man with a deep voice who also may seem frightening to you. But look closely and you will see the kindness in his soul. He is your father. He is the one who has given me the courage to fight for you, through all the struggles to free you from the myriads of paperwork and tangled connections that have trapped you for so long. This man is a champion of lost causes. He is tenacious. He is loving. You will now have a voice. Take his hand.

I understand the enormity of what you are about to do. It must terrify you to leave so much behind. My eyes fill with tears when I think of you leaving your homeland, a country I have come to love and revere. But there are many things you can bring with you from China. Bring your pride in your heritage; you are part of one of the oldest civilizations in the world. Bring your memories of the incredible forest that surrounds you. Bring with you the admirable Chinese traits of hard work, honesty, and respect for elders. Bring with you thoughts of the beauty and majesty of your ancestral home. Bring with you love for the orphanage directors who so desperately tried to find you a family. Bring memories of friends that became your chosen family. Bring with you the indomitable spirit that sustained you through all the disappointments you endured.

But there are many things to leave behind. Leave behind the hunger that has been your companion for so long that you could not even put down your bowl of rice for a minute to have your picture taken. Leave behind the endless cold and darkness you have known. Leave behind your need. As long as I have breath in my body, you will never want again. I wish that I could ask you to leave behind the sadness that causes you to walk with your head down. Let me help you carry that burden of sorrow. Take my hand.

If you only knew how many nights I've looked up and thought about you awaking under the same sky on the other side of the world. If you could only know how much I've come to love you; how sure I am that you are my very own daughter. I knew it from the start. The very first time I saw your waiting face, almost two years ago now, I knew with certainty that you and I were mother and daughter. And I believed it even when I was told over and over by different authorities that you were not available for adoption, that you had already been placed. You have never been out of my prayers. Even before I knew your name, I asked God for guardian angels to watch over "the little girl in the green coat." He knew whom I meant. For unlike what many say about adoption, I did not choose you. God chose us for each other.

Unthinking people may tell you in the future that we saved your life. They are mistaken. You saved your own life. You chose life under conditions that cause others to choose to give up. You held on to hope. It buoyed you through the rough seas you have already traveled. In celebration of your new life, and the triumph of hope it represents, your new American middle name will be Hope. May it serve always as a reminder of how remarkable your journey has been.

I don't know what your future holds, but I can promise you this: I will try to be worthy of your trust. I will cherish your homeland and continue to celebrate its traditions with you. I will try to instill in you pride and joy so that you walk, from this time on, with your head held high. I have learned a few lessons from parenting already. I know how important it is to let you forge your own path. And whether you grow up to be a bus driver or a ballerina, I will rejoice in your success. And when you fall, I will be there to catch you, dust you off, and put you back in the race. Because my blood doesn't run in your veins, I will not be searching your face for some reflection of myself. You will be free to be who you are. And, most importantly, you will always have love. Take my hand.

Let me tell you about your new family. In addition to adoring parents, you will have a big sister, Kate, who is like no other. When I first showed your picture to her, she looked at it and said simply, "I see a little girl who needs a mommy and a daddy." When I told her all the changes in her life this would mean, and all the sharing that would be involved, she looked at me solemnly and said, "But Mom, that's what it is to be a big sister!" She then went upstairs and started dividing up her dresser drawers. Kate peered anxiously at your shaved head in the recent photo and asked me if we should keep you home from school until your hair grew. I told her this was not possible. The next day she marched into school and sternly warned the kindergartners that they were not to tease her sister. She will have to move on to first grade, but she will be there to watch over her sister in the summer. I have a feeling she will be your protector and greatest confidante all the days of your life and long after my time on this earth is over. She will share your secrets. She will hold your hand in the dark. Take her hand.

And then there is the irrepressible imp we named Christy. She's the one who will grab your toys, clunk around in your too-big shoes, and crumple your treasures. She is so mischievous that Kate worried that Santa was going to bring her a lump of coal. But she is easy to love; her charm is hard to resist. She is like a walking ray of sunshine. I suspect that in short order you'll be begging her for kisses like the rest of us. And she shares your homeland, a bond that transcends blood. She will most assuredly reach out her tiny hand to you. Take it.

And this is only the beginning of the family and dear friends we have waiting for you here in America. You have already touched so many hearts. Countless prayers have been offered for your homecoming.

Come, begin the wonderful adventure of your future. I will be right beside you every step of the way. Take my hand.

Love,
Mom

The Waiting Child

Chapter One

The First Meeting

Fear grows out of the things we think; it lives in our minds. Compassion grows out
of the things we are, and lives in our hearts.
—Barbara Garrison

We sat stiffly on the edge of the couch in the Office of Civil Affairs in the city of Gualing, China. It was a warm day near the end of June 1999. The office was small and dingy, with peeling paint on the wall, age-streaked tile, and a hodgepodge of mismatched furnishings. Hallways were filled to the brim with an unusual stockpile of miscellaneous merchandise, making movement through them nearly impossible. Everything was covered in dust; it was all filthy. It was an inauspicious place for such a momentous occasion.

Our guide whispered, "I think they're here." We could hear the rustle from the hallway of someone approaching. Here it was, the moment we had awaited for over two years: our first meeting with our new daughter. A middle-aged Chinese woman wearing old-fashioned glasses entered the room. She had a firm grasp on a small child. It was Lou Jiao. Finally. This was the child we had traveled halfway around the world to meet. The one we had moved heaven and earth for. The one whose picture had haunted me for what seemed like forever. The one for whom I had silently prayed for so long. My daughter. My first thought was that she looked exactly like her photo. Her eyes had the same frightened expression as in the picture. They made her appear much older and wiser than her almost four years. Those were the eyes that had haunted me for so long. They made me feel as if I knew who she was already, as if I could read the sorrow in her heart.

She looked at me with a sideways glance, her head bowed. She seemed terrified. Her hair was shorn close to her head in a typical orphanage hairstyle. Her nose was running, and she was holding, without any feeling of attachment, a teddy bear wearing an American flag sweater that we had sent to her. Her face had some visible scarring. On first impression she looked somewhat larger than I had expected, maybe because of the size of her dress. It was made of thin, cheap cotton in a bright pattern of red and yellow. It looked like a dress that might be purchased at a garage sale in a poor community in the United States. I am certain that it represented the best dress the orphanage had to put on her for her big day. She had on dingy, gray-that-once-were-white silk socks and red felt shoes. She glanced at me shyly with her head still down.

A young woman who appeared to be no more than twenty years old followed her. She was slight, with the short hairstyle favored by the more modern young Chinese women. She wore heavy, thick glasses that slipped down her tiny nose. She seemed to be urging Lou Jiao on from behind. The older woman locked eyes with me and firmly pulled Lou Jiao over to the black vinyl sofa where I was anxiously perched. Rick tried valiantly to videotape this first meeting. The woman began to cajole Lou Jiao by insisting that she sit next to me and call me "Mama." The frightened child sat as close to the woman as she could. I found out months later that Lou Jiao had never met this older woman before this day; she worked in the office and was unknown to the children. But she was at least Chinese, and this must have seemed like something to cling to when the fair-haired stranger now before her reached out her hands. She did allow me to wipe her nose; it was my first official act as her mother. I tried to smile brightly and realized that my tears were fewer and less heartfelt than when I had adopted my baby, Christy, just a year ago. I tried valiantly to put a smile on my fear. Lou Jiao did not even try.

Around us, surveying this scene with trepidation, were a host of others. Our Chinese guide, Emily, tried to speak brightly to the officials and to the representatives of the orphanage. She was a young woman with a pretty face and a pleasant manner. Her long, silky hair caught the rays of light that peeked through the grime-caked windows. She was casually dressed in Western jeans and a denim jacket. She seemed anxious for things to go well.

Before Lou Jiao arrived, Emily had conferred with the orphanage staff by phone. She then told us that the child's arrival had been delayed because Lou Jiao didn't want to get in the car to come here. But when Emily saw my stricken face, she laughed artificially and quickly revised the story; she said she was just kidding. Events later seemed to confirm the first version of events. Then, after another phone conversation, she reported that the arrival would be delayed because Lou Jiao had gotten carsick on the trip. After our rush to arrive at this drab government office, the half-hour delay gave us a chance to start on the paperwork and, more importantly, to catch our breath. But my apprehension and fear had grown with each passing minute.

Several Chinese government workers were busy with the required paperwork. They tried to stay unobtrusively in the background. Later, I had trouble recalling anything about them, even their gender. They were polite and efficient. They stayed by their desks and out of the way of the reception area where we were seated. The paperwork, which had seemed so momentous during our first adoption, was mundane and routine this time. We answered routine questions before Lou Jiao arrived and signed our names to various forms as directed by Emily. Now that we knew the expected answers, there were no difficult questions. And, to be frank, almost no real interest in our answers.

As we were the only parents being processed at this time, the paperwork flowed without any delays. But we missed the camaraderie of having others to share our special moment. We were alone for the "birth" of this child.

We were all relying on Emily's translation for the important task of communication. Without her words, we would be lost. I incorrectly assumed that the older woman was the assistant director of the orphanage. She turned out to be the bookkeeper. She was there for the sole purpose of getting our three-thousand-dollar cash donation and making sure it was safely deposited at the bank. She seemed in a hurry, impatient to transact this business and leave. The money, a "required donation," must be presented in crisp new American hundred-dollar bills. She accepted it on trust without counting it. To us, it was a small price to pay. To those entrusted with the care and feeding of over three hundred children, it was a small fortune. Although some witnessing such a transaction—where a child is turned over in exchange for money—might view the money as payment or ransom for the child, we saw it differently. It was our gift. It was reimbursement for the food, lodging, and care our daughter had received from the orphanage for the last two years. It was a totally inadequate gesture to those who had literally saved her life.

I began my attempt at winning over the child with a strategy that had served me well with children in the past: bribery. I opened my bag and got out a package of animal crackers and offered her one. She immediately accepted it from me and shoved the whole cracker in her mouth. She was now more interested in me or, more accurately, in what I had. I was ready to surrender the whole package, but Emily told me that the bookkeeper had asked that I not feed the child. She had just been carsick, after all, and they did not want her to vomit again. I felt defeated; I knew that food was key to making this first connection.

The bookkeeper continued cajoling Lou Jiao and physically tried to shove her closer to me on the couch. In response, Lou Jiao pushed closer to the woman, although she did not put out her arms toward the woman or attempt to touch her. She did not cry. She just stared. Over and over the woman demanded, with increasing insistence, that the child call me "Mama" until Lou Jiao finally squeaked out the word. It was painful to behold. This was not what I wanted, this unnatural forcing of the bond between mother and child. I understood her terror and her shyness; I had no expectations of her. But I was powerless to stop the badgering; she was not yet mine. I was a stranger in a strange land, so I had to follow their lead.

The bookkeeper finally surrendered her place next to Lou Jiao, and the younger woman, who we learned was Lou Jiao's teacher, talked to her in a quiet, coaxing manner. Lou Jiao clearly trusted her and seemed to feel comfortable with her. It was evident that the child had no interest in the American teddy bear she was holding. I found out later that she had never seen it before the car ride. It was the policy of the orphanage for the children to have no ownership of possessions, for each child to share equally in all. So, although they had brought the bear today because they knew we had sent it to her, she had had no opportunity to form an attachment to it. I had hoped that to her it would represent her new family and home, but it represented nothing.

I continued my bribery strategy by bringing out the doll I had carefully selected for the occasion. Lou Jiao accepted it immediately and began to brush its hair with the tiny hairbrush I handed her. As she sat closer to me, she brought up one tentative finger to touch my hair and then quickly pulled it back. I had worried that she would be taken aback by my fair complexion and blond looks, but she did not seem to be. Finally she was close enough for us to be able to take some "first meeting" photos without a wide-angle lens. We took one with her, the schoolteacher, and me. We took one with Lou Jiao, her new dad, and me. We were smiling; she was not. It felt forced and phony to all of us, but we knew it was truly a huge moment that deserved to be recorded.

We continued to speak through Emily. I pulled out a long list of questions I had for the orphanage staff. This might be my only chance to find out anything about my new daughter and her past. Emily studied the list and then decided that this was not the time to tackle these questions. It was now Monday. She promised that we would be able to visit the orphanage on Wednesday and would then have an opportunity to have our questions answered. We agreed to wait for these answers and were pleased that she was confirming that we would be able to visit the orphanage. This was always a question mark in China. The adverse publicity about conditions in the orphanages had virtually closed them to Western visitors. We knew we were once again being afforded a rare privilege. We also knew that our visit was allowed only because this orphanage was considered a showplace in China. It was one of the very few that had been permitted to receive financial support from charitable organizations outside China.

Emily seemed in a hurry to conclude this meeting. She surreptitiously checked the paperwork and answered the questions posed by the officials with minimal involvement from us. At one point the officials approached Lou Jiao with a red ink pad and placed her fingerprint on the documents. That was it: her seal, her signature of acceptance of this adoption. She had no voice in the process and was unaware of the significance of what she was doing.

Even now it is hard to describe the emotions I felt during this first meeting. I was not basking in the sheer beauty of my new daughter, as I had when I adopted Christy; this seemed more like taking inventory. Also missing was the rush of mother's love that had filled me last time. Although I told Lou Jiao from the start that I loved her—it was one of the few Chinese phrases I could say—it was a lie. I did not yet feel any real connection to her. What I felt most keenly was fear. I was sweating, uncertain, and felt that things were spinning out of control, that time was moving too quickly; I was not ready for this. A strange jumble of emotions surged through me, but one thing I knew with certainty: joy wasn't one of them.

I finally got her close enough to pull her onto my lap. She sat there stiffly. I was surprised at how heavy she seemed. I was sure she weighed more than the thirty-five pounds that I had been told she weighed. I worried that all the clothes I had so carefully selected for her would be too small. I tried to show her the button I was wearing. I had worn it on all my clothes for days now. It was a picture of her with the words *I love Lou Jiao* across the bottom. I hoped it would help her understand that she belonged to me. She studied it with puzzlement.

She did look with me at the black Mickey Mouse photo book she had brought with her. It was one I had sent ahead in the box with the teddy bear and two disposable cameras. It was filled with pictures of our family and home. We'd had a Chinese friend add captions under the photos explaining who was in each one, in hopes that someone would review the book with her in preparation for her adoption. She paged through it, studying each picture with intensity, and shyly looked back at me as if to confirm that I was the woman in the photos. Although I had no idea of the extent of her preparation, or how long she had known we were coming, she had definitely seen these pictures before. In fact, I was surprised when we actually got home weeks later and she was able to show me things in our home that were now different than they had been in the photos. As I did not yet know the term *hypervigilance*, the term psychologists use to identify the heightened state of awareness that children who have suffered abuse possess, I concluded that she was very bright. In any event, she had obviously studied these photos intently.

As we flipped through the book, I directed Emily to our gift bags. As is the Chinese custom, we had brought red gift bags as gratuities and a means of thanking each of the government workers. The bags were filled with American-made trinkets that are scarcities in China—cosmetics, nail polish, T-shirts, and hats with American logos. Emily distributed them discreetly, and the government employees slid them into their desks without glancing at the contents. This is their custom; gifts are given without fanfare and never opened in the presence of the giver.

The young teacher had brought with her the two disposable cameras we had mailed in advance of our visit. We had enclosed a letter asking that they be used to take photos of Lou Jiao, her surroundings, and her friends. We knew that the government forbade the taking of photographs inside orphanages since the bout of bad publicity a few years earlier. Given this, we were prepared to have empty cameras returned to us or to discover that the letter and instructions had not been understood. We were surprised when the teacher indicated that she had finished one camera off and that the second one had only a few pictures left. Rick and I exchanged hopeful glances. We then asked the teacher if these cameras had any pictures of Jin Xun Li, Lou Jiao's best friend, whom my sister Laura had been trying desperately to adopt for the last year. She smiled and said, "Of course. Lots of pictures of Jin Xun Li." Rick and I were thrilled with this news. We had been worried about what had happened to her, since my sister had recently been told that she could not adopt her. We became hopeful; if she was still there, maybe there was still a possibility that Laura could adopt this child that we had all loved for so long.

We had been in the dingy government office for about an hour. Lou Jiao, due to her late arrival, had only been with us half an hour. It felt like much longer. I had to ask Rick later if she was now adopted; I had no idea of her status or what had just occurred legally. We began to move toward the door. All was well. Lou Jiao went with us without protest and even held my proffered hand as we descended four dark flights of filthy, crumbling stairs. I began to feel hopeful. Maybe this wouldn't be as difficult as I thought.

The orphanage staff walked down the stairs behind us with Emily bringing up the rear. Mrs. Hong, our Chinese driver, was waiting in the car for us. We made our way through a dirty, dimly lit hallway and down a crumbling outdoor staircase and were back out in the bright sun. It was now late afternoon. We all walked over to the car, where the orphanage staff said a cursory good-bye to Lou Jiao. They did not stop to embrace her; they barely slowed down on the way to their car.

As she saw the staff prepare to leave, Lou Jiao stopped walking. She pulled her hand from mine and planted her feet firmly about four feet away from our car. She was not budging. And she had begun to cry. The orphanage staff swooped in to put an end to this display. They began urging her again in earnest and directed a furious volley of Chinese words at her. I had no idea what they were saying and stood there mute and helpless, unsure of what to do. Both Emily and our driver added their voices to the melee cajoling Lou Jiao to get into the car. She was not budging. Her crying had turned to screams, which increased in pitch and intensity as the cajoling continued. It seemed that she was no longer even aware of what was being said to her. Her screams became rhythmic, like the enraged reaction of an animal that has been cornered and can't break free. It was a sound I had never heard before in my life and hope never to hear again: the sound of pure human agony. I stood there unsure of what to do next, trying to gently guide her into the car. Finally, Rick came over from the other side of the car, picked her up, and bodily folded her into the backseat. This was the point at which it began to feel as if a kidnapping were taking place. Ignoring her screams, the orphanage staff quickly walked away. Emily and our driver jumped into the car, and we were off in a hurry.

Lou Jiao was lying stiffly across my lap as I attempted to hold her on the small backseat. Emily and Mrs. Hong kept up the furious cajoling in Chinese. Emily turned around in her front passenger seat and gently tapped Lou Jiao on the leg while repeating "Jiao, Jiao" over and over in an attempt to get her attention. Lou Jiao was in her own world; the rhythmic screaming, at the highest possible decibel of sound, continued without abatement. We made our way through the late afternoon traffic, the windows tightly sealed to keep the sound in, and the driver reluctantly turned on the car's air-conditioning to compensate for the closed windows. Bikes scattered all around our car as it wove aggressively through several lanes of heavy traffic that seemed to move in random patterns. I was focused on trying to get Lou Jiao to soften into the folds of my body and let me comfort her. It was impossible. There truly was no comforting her. So deep was her grief that she had sealed off her soul from the rest of humanity.

The drive to the hotel took about twenty minutes; it seemed much longer. Emily tried to maintain her cheery smile and give us instructions about our itinerary for tomorrow as if nothing out of the ordinary was going on. It was nearly impossible to hear anything she said. The driver pulled up abruptly in front of our hotel and opened the car door to help us out. Lou Jiao was unmoving and unseeing, her eyes shut as the tears poured from them. Rick came over and again lifted her in his arms. As he briskly carried her through the lobby of the lush four-star hotel, its lofty ceilings and huge open spaces reverberated with the sound of the child's screams. We tried desperately to appear nonchalant to those standing and staring. I truly didn't see those who were gawking; I was focused on escaping this very public debacle. Inside me was an element of fear that one of those observing might worry about what was being done to the child. I wondered if it would be possible in the United States for two foreigners to forcibly carry a child through a hotel lobby, one who was so clearly unwilling to go with them, without someone calling the authorities.

She continued to scream, her body stiff, all the way up in the elevator and down the long hall to our room. She would not be comforted. In the room I sat down on one of the beds, and Rick placed her in my lap. She was unseeing. She just screamed and screamed. She did not respond to my arms around her or allow herself to lean against me.

I turned to Rick and asked, "What do you think we should do now?"

"Well," he said reasonably, "we have no idea how long this might go on. We have to be prepared for the possibility that she could scream all night. I'm anxious to see if I can get the pictures that the orphanage took developed. We have to see if Jin Xun Li is really still there. Maybe we should take shifts staying here with her."

I agreed, knowing that it was the rational thing to do, but as I watched him leave I felt a rising sense of panic. My parenting instincts were not the strongest even in the best of circumstances; I had absolutely no idea what I should do next. I tried everything. I talked to her softly. I sang to her. I took out the tiny set of cards I had with the phonetic pronunciations of Chinese phrases on them. I attempted to say some reassuring phrases in Chinese, like "It will be all right. Don't be afraid." Nothing worked. I had no idea how long she had been screaming, as time had taken on a surreal quality for me. It seemed like forever. In reality it was probably no more than an hour. Then, finally, she stopped. I found myself eyeball to eyeball with her, now my legally adopted daughter, and it suddenly hit me: my long sought-after child was a complete stranger. To my surprise, there was nothing familiar about her at all.

She continued to allow me to wipe her nose. And now that we were on my turf, I started with the bribes again. I had a supply of snacks that I had brought with me to try to win her over. My extensive reading on the adoption of older institutionalized children had taught me that food equated security for these kids. This seemed to be true in her case. Although she did not appear to be malnourished, her security need proved to be very great. Every snack I produced she grabbed. She opened, without assistance, the small packages of cookies and crackers I produced, but limited her immediate consumption to one or two that she quickly jammed into her mouth as if to protect them from being snatched back. She then carefully closed the package and began to create a stash. She watched where I was getting the food from, then went to those spots unassisted and grabbed the remaining snacks to add to her stash, which she hovered over protectively. I realized then that this was a bad idea; I was afraid she would overeat and make herself sick. I was also surprised by the bold way she snatched things without seeking my permission; my children would never have done such a thing. I never even stopped to consider how ridiculous it was that I should think this child would react the way my children would. I surreptitiously hid the remaining food.

Seeking to find a connection, I grabbed the photo album that had so enchanted her and we looked at it together. I tried to say the Chinese words to identify our family members' relationships to her. I continued to try to say the Chinese phrases from the little cards. She looked at me in puzzlement as I did this and finally grabbed the cards herself and studied them as if to ask, "Why does she keep looking at these?" She was silent. She clearly understood that I couldn't comprehend her words, and she made it clear through her confused expressions that she could not understand mine. Even if my Chinese pronunciation had been better, she was from a province where they spoke a distinctive dialect that was different from both Mandarin and Cantonese. To supplement the photos in the album, I pulled out a tiny photo album that I always carried in my purse. Inside were pictures of her with her orphanage best friend, Jin Xun Li. These were the pictures that kept us going through the myriad obstacles in the journey to becoming her parents. These photos elicited her first smile. Her eyes widened in delight as she recognized herself and her friend. "Jin Xun Li!" she said with excitement as she pointed to her friend.

I had also packed a bright pink Barbie backpack of toys for her. I hid the backpack in the closet so as to not overwhelm her with all these riches at once. After all, she had not until this day ever owned anything. In keeping with the Communist philosophy, each child in the orphanage shared and shared alike with any toys or clothes. We saw firsthand how this worked later in the week when we visited the orphanage. One child wore an outfit one day. At night it was taken off and placed on a rail outside the rooms. The first one to grab it in the morning wore it the next day. That is, if someone else didn't grab it away from them. The weakest or the slowest ended up wearing flannel nightgowns as dresses on hot days in June. And this was the practice with everything. We found out later that in the part of the institution where Lou Jiao lived, there were no toys. These were reserved for children that were registered for adoption; Lou Jiao had been considered hard to place and was not among those lucky few.

She watched every movement I made with open curiosity, taking careful note of where I was going to retrieve each item. Once again her obvious hypervigilance was on display; I did not know then that the behavior was symptomatic of abuse. I continued to believe that she was simply bright and curious.

To my surprise, she was not shy in exploring her new environment. Almost immediately she went to my open suitcase and started foraging. She grabbed a bra and studied it with fascination. It was clear that she had never seen one before and did not know what it was. She studied it from various angles. She also clutched my bathing suit, pulled it out, and held it up to herself. It, too, was a novelty, and I could see her puzzlement over what this strange item of clothing could possibly be. Instead of being amused, I was put off by her lack of boundaries. Who was this child who felt so comfortable rooting through a stranger's suitcase? I tried to redirect her attention, but she would have none of it. She wanted to explore her surroundings on her own terms. She was entirely different from the shy child I expected. Finally, Rick returned. I was never so happy to see anyone in my life. Although he had been gone only a short time, it seemed forever.

"I found a photo place and was able to negotiate a price by passing a calculator back and forth. How's she doing?" he said in one breath. "At least she isn't screaming anymore."

My relief made my knees weak and I sank to the floor. I·tried to relate to him bits and pieces of the eternity that had just passed, as my fear, held in check while I was "in charge," came churning back. Lou Jiao had introduced me to an emotion I had never known before: the heart-stopping, choking, sick-to-your-stomach kind of fear, the run-while-you-still-can-and-never-look-back kind. Waves of nausea washed over me. I had the sensation that I was going to jump out of my skin.

"Rick," I said, "I have never been so terrified in my life. I honestly feel like I'm going to vomit." He looked at me in confusion. So sure was I of his answer that I dared to ask, "Are you scared?"

"Yes," he said with complete candor. This was not the answer I had anticipated and it made me feel suddenly much worse. Rick, experienced from raising his own children, was so much better with kids than I was, I just assumed that he would feel completely in control of a strange four-year-old. After all, this was his sixth child. He had been a capable parent for more than thirty years. In comparison, I was still a rookie.

"What are you afraid of?" I asked.

"All my fear is for her," he said with tear-filled eyes. "If we feel like this, how in the world must she feel?"

Yes, she was the child. I was the adult. Then why did she seem so much more capable of handling this than I? I knew that all my thoughts should be about making it easier for her, but I was paralyzed by the enormity of what lay before me. It was too big. Or, more truthfully, I was too small. Although I never once seriously thought of giving her back, if there had been some graceful way to get out of there and go back home, I'm not so sure I wouldn't have snatched it. I thought of all those who had said how brave I was to do an older child adoption; I was thankful that they couldn't see me now.

Sensing the depth of my fear, Rick immediately took over and began playing with her. I sat and watched. He began showing her all her new clothes. She seemed to love the hats and carefully examined each item of clothing. In spite of my worries, they all fit her. She delighted in some, but did not let us hold them too close to her, as she obviously did not want to take her shoes or clothes off.

She looked in wonder at the toilet; she clearly had never seen one. I gave her a little demonstration, and she mastered this novelty in no time. I marveled at the quickest toilet training ever. She later flushed a bracelet down the toilet and peeked under the lid periodically for its return. When it didn't reappear, she finally understood how this new contraption worked.

After a while we ventured out to take her to dinner at the hotel restaurant, and she willingly took our hands. She looked around in fascination at this new room. The restaurant had a breathtaking view of the city. The staff brought a booster chair for her and she cooperatively climbed into it. I didn't know what to order for her, so I chose a Chinese chicken dish. She brightened noticeably when the food came and shoveled it into her mouth with astonishing speed. But she wasn't nearly as interested in her Chinese food as she was in our french fries and catsup. She pointed to Rick's Coke and he offered her a sip.

"This kid's ready for America," Rick said with a laugh as she downed the whole can.

She began to talk to us haltingly, as if forgetting that we could not understand her. She would not answer the Chinese strangers who approached our table and tried to talk to her.

After dinner I bravely decided to tackle giving Lou Jiao her first bath. As there is some inherent sense of vulnerability in shedding one's clothes—in this case, all she owned in the world—I expected a battle, but to my surprise she made no difficulty. I had noticed that she washed her hands with the vigor and thoroughness of a surgeon, and placed in the tub she immediately began quickly scrubbing her body in the same methodical manner. I stopped her from rubbing the bar soap roughly on her head and introduced her to shampoo. Then, trying to add some childish fun, I threw a small beach ball into the tub with her. Lou Jiao, not understanding, began to scrub it, too.

When she finished scrubbing herself and the ball, I let the water out. She grabbed the washcloth and began to scour the tub. Then she capably wrung out the washcloth and hung it neatly to dry. I could not believe I was watching a child; her competence belied her years. She then gestured for me to get into the tub and began to run my bath. After I climbed in, she handed me the shampoo and then threw the ball in for me.

Lou Jiao willingly climbed into the bed I indicated and looked at me with forlorn eyes. As she studied my face intently, she reached one tiny hand out toward me. I held it, and we lay together, each wary of the other. Hoping to comfort her, I brought to her the photos of her former life that Rick had developed earlier. She slowly and carefully examined each one, saying her friends' names over and over. Rick and I marveled at the gift we had been given: pictures of her in her classroom, her bed, washing up in the morning, and at mealtime with her friends. As we got to the last photo in the album, a shot of me holding her on my lap earlier in the day, Lou Jiao pointed to it and softly said, "Mama," while she looked directly into my eyes.

And suddenly it hit me: I was Lou Jiao's mama. Finally.

Chapter Two

Getting to Know You

The gem cannot be polished without friction, nor man perfected without trials.
—Chinese proverb

Each subsequent day began the way that first day had ended. As soon as Lou Jiao awoke, she wanted to look at the photos of her old friends. It was clear that she longed for them. Over and over she would call me over and point to one child in particular. His name sounded like "Xiao Mei Mei," and I had noticed that she often called this name out in her sleep, too. She would become distraught when she looked at his somber little face. The child was unbelievably pathetic. He reminded me of a concentration camp survivor.

She was thrilled with her new wardrobe and would willingly dress in the clothes I had selected. She slipped on her Mickey Mouse underpants with delight and carefully practiced walking in her new saddle shoes. But what she loved most was the clear novelty of her new hats. I had brought hats to try to disguise the hacked-off brush cut that was the standard orphanage style; her hair was so badly cropped it appeared that a drunken sailor had held the scissors. But then again, what could I have expected when hair had to be cut so often for so many children, to protect them from lice.

Once Emily arrived to take us to the day's destination, Lou Jiao would visibly brighten. She loved exploring the city as much as we did. The first time we were in China, we had timidly made our way through the street markets. Some in our travel group could barely disguise their revulsion at the sights. Tiny booths crammed into small alleys held a diverse and often bizarre display of goods, from high-tech cameras and DVDs to herbs for medicinal purposes. Snakes coiled in the bottom of wine jugs, while monkeys, cats, and dogs were offered as gourmet dinners. Eels and live turtles squirmed in bins everywhere: these were not sights for the weak of heart. On our previous trip, "How interesting!" was our most enthusiastic response. But this time, seeing it all through Lou Jiao's eyes, we could hardly get enough of the street scenes. The number of people on the street was astounding in and of itself. Pedestrians packed every sidewalk. Bicycles, sometimes ten deep, rode alongside cars, buses, and motorcycles. Traffic moved aggressively with very few traffic signals; horns blared constantly, but amazingly few accidents occurred. Contemporary state-of-the-art chrome and glass office buildings were juxtaposed with crumbling, filthy ghettolike housing. Everywhere the old and the new, side by side, provided a stark contrast between China's rich history and its huge strides toward westernizing. Some of it saddened me. I relished the thought of a civilization that was so old and felt remorse when I saw work crews tearing down the intricately carved structures with their vibrant colors and distinctively Asian flavor.

The cornucopia of sights, sounds, and smells was something to revel in; they were wondrous. And if we were in awe, Lou Jiao was nearly in orbit. She told us, through Emily, of course, that she had never been allowed outside the gates of the orphanage. She was not shy about going over to any crowd of people she saw on the street and pushing forward to see what they were all so interested in. She was fascinated by simply everything, and it was a joy to watch her delight. She acted as if she had just been freed; she couldn't get enough of the sights.

Feeling slightly more confident with each new day, we decided that it was time to begin acclimating Lou Jiao to her new life by calling her by an American name. We knew that orphanage children generally had assigned names, chosen at random, and assuming that the same was true for Lou Jiao, we had decided not to retain any of it but to name her Jaclyn, after my favorite aunt. Since the surname comes first in China, her first name was really Jiao and her last Lou. Jiao Lou and Jaclyn seemed close enough to make an easy change. I wanted her to feel like an American in her new life and felt that an American name would help her assimilate and be less conspicuous in a group of peers.

Emily was vital to any explanation.

"Emily, we want you to ask Lou Jiao if we could call her Jaclyn," I directed. "Could you tell her that Lou Jiao translates to Jaclyn in America?" We didn't feel any concern over this white lie, as we believed that we needed to offer some logical explanation for the change. Emily agreed to the request with a stone-faced glance. Her chilling response seemed curious to me given the fact that she had chosen the name Emily for herself when she was with Americans. In fact, she never even told us her Chinese name. But with obvious disapproval, Emily knelt down and spoke to the child. Lou Jiao nodded numbly that she understood. We smiled happily at her as we pronounced her Jaclyn, oblivious to her pain. We truly believed that we were doing the right thing. I could not understand then what that nod of assent had cost the child. Only much later did I realize what an insensitive blunder I had made; in truth, the name that I ripped away and discarded so cavalierly was the only remnant of her birth family that she carried with her.

Emily refused to call her Jaclyn even after I begged her to do so. But Jaclyn was shrewd, and she knew how to curry favor with us; she was a survivor. Later that day she made a point of pointing to Rick and me as she distinctively said "*Baba*" (the Chinese word for "dad") and "Mama." Then, to our surprise, she pointed to herself and said, "JACK-WIN!" We clapped enthusiastically in response. I had no understanding of how difficult this must have been for her and was simply delighted with her compliance.

Each day, Jaclyn became increasingly bold in her misbehavior. She would suddenly refuse to walk and would flop on the ground laughing. She would demand potato chips and pitch a tantrum when they were not purchased for her. I would have put an end to these antics quickly, as Rick and I both believed it was important even now to set limits for her, but it was impossible with Emily handling the mothering. Jaclyn would only hold Emily's hand. The two of them often went off together, leaving Rick and me twenty paces behind.

Jaclyn had now established that she could get away with any conduct with Emily, who laughed and encouraged all her bad behavior. As the days wore on, Jaclyn began spinning out of control, as any child without limits does.

Emily was eager to share with us some of China's folklore, so she brought us to a local park that displayed a series of about thirty murals in a large hall. She dragged us inside and began telling us very detailed stories about the fables depicted by each mural. We were politely feigning interest when Rick looked around and realized with a start that Jaclyn was gone. Only a parent can understand the rush of panic that I felt; bile rose in my throat and I could feel my heart clench. We raced out of the hall in three different directions, frantically calling her name. There was no answer. She was nowhere in sight. The park was huge— acres of land with a deep lake in the middle. Could she have fallen in? Where could she have gone? I realized with a start that heavy traffic flowed in lanes three deep surrounding the park. Had she left the park and run away? I ran, screaming her name frantically, searching everywhere while my heart pounded furiously in my chest. How could I have made a mistake like this—how could I have let her get away? Oh, God, please keep her safe, I prayed silently over and over. After about ten excruciating minutes, I found her hiding under a park bench. She was all giggles, and the only one laughing harder than her was Emily. Even though her disappearance had saved us from the incredibly boring murals, Rick and I were both livid.

Fear gave me courage, and the showdown between the dueling mothers began.

"Emily," I said in a voice shaking with anger, "this has to stop now. I am her mother, and I have to have the authority to make rules for Jaclyn for her own safety. In America, children that are not with an adult can be abducted in a park. Her behavior is totally unacceptable to us! What Jaclyn did was dangerous. I insist that you tell her that!" Emily was obviously miffed by both my lecture and my tone. She shook her head firmly, indicating her refusal to scold Jaclyn, protesting by saying over and over, "She's too young."

But I was not willing to give in this time. I continued to insist that she translate my words. Finally yielding to my insistence, Emily huffed in annoyance, "Well, this expected behavior of children must be different in America than it is in China." This fueled the fire of my rage even more.

"Emily, you know that is not true. I have seen many Chinese moms with their children; I know they are very strict. I never see other children acting up the way Jaclyn does!" It was hard to refute this, so Emily was silent.

The upshot of our angry words, all spoken in English so that Jaclyn could not understand them, was that Jaclyn spurned us. She would only hold hands with her dear friend Emily, who clearly was superior in every way to these horrid parents who wanted her to obey. We walked through the rest of the park in stony silence.

When we got to the exit, Jaclyn decided that she did not want to hold anyone's hand to cross the four-lane road to the parking lot. There were no pedestrian walkways, and cars, bikes, and motorcycles were flying by at incredible speeds. I managed to grab Jaclyn before she set foot in traffic and physically wrestled with her, barely able to maintain my grip, as we crossed the road. As soon as we got to the parking lot, she fled into the arms and comfort of the waiting driver, Mrs. Hong. Emily, too, could hardly wait to see Mrs. Hong, and immediately began an animated discussion with her about what had occurred. Although the venting was all in Chinese, as Mrs. Hong did not speak English, it was apparent that she was talking about us. It was hard to hear any conversation very well in the car, however, as Mrs. Hong, like all good Chinese drivers, drove with one hand continually on the horn.

The morning had been an unmitigated disaster. I could not imagine the horror of our next step: the final good-bye between Jaclyn and her orphanage friends. In preparation for it, we went back to the hotel where I began to sort and package the clothes I had brought to donate to the orphanage. Seeming to understand what I was doing, Jaclyn took all the smallest items from my hands and put them into a separate pile. "Xiao Mei Mei," she would say lovingly as she carefully folded each tiny item. Rick and I became increasingly apprehensive as the time for departure approached. I knew rationally that Jaclyn had to have some closure and a chance to say a final good-bye to all her old friends. But given how things were going with her, I feared that she would not want to leave with us again and that we would have a replay of the kidnapping scenario of the first day. I didn't know if I could go through that again.

Almost as if she could sense my unhappiness, Jaclyn turned to me and said "*Xie xie* [thank you], Mama," indicating the pile of clothing she had put aside for Xiao Mei Mei. The selflessness of her heartfelt gratitude took me completely by surprise. Who was this fierce but empathetic child? I wondered as I watched her struggle to pack up her precious bundle.

Chapter Three

The First Farewell

A part of you has grown in me . . . we may be apart in distance, but never in heart.
—Unknown

We tried hard to swallow our trepidation as we got into the car. We asked Emily to emphasize to Jaclyn that she was not going back to the orphanage to live. She did so and indicated that Jaclyn understood this.

On the drive there we got a cell phone call from Julie Kerr, staff coordinator in China of the Great Wall China Adoption agency. Once we had discovered that Jin Xun Li was still in the orphanage, we had asked her to check again on her availability for adoption. Julie was full of apologies but said definitely that Jin Xun Li had already been referred to a different family. This still seemed suspect to us. We had been told this months ago. Why was she still in the orphanage? I trusted Julie implicitly and knew she had done everything possible to help these best friends get adopted together. To make up for our disappointment, Julie indicated that the China Center for Adoption Affairs had authorized the Gualing orphanage to register for adoption an additional five children over their annual quota in the requested age range. Out of these five, Julie would work with them to select a child for Laura and Jeff. We were pleased that at least Jaclyn's new cousin would be from her orphanage. Since it was known as one of the better orphanages in China, we were also reassured to know that this new addition would have had the benefit of good care.

Although I loved Julie and knew she had done her best, the news was still like a blow to the gut. It's funny how attached you can become to a child from photos and a few scraps of information about them. Little did I realize that this feeling of loss would pale in comparison with the grief I felt after I met Jin Xun Li.

We headed down a long alleyway, following the arrow from a sign on the main thoroughfare. We were almost breathless when the first glimpse of the orphanage came into view. The building was enormous with several floors and sprawling wings. The white tile that surrounded it made it appear clean and bright. Blue and red peaked spires and brightly colored trim made it appear like a children's castle. If an institution could look charming, this one did.

A teacher was walking with a large group of disabled toddlers on the grass bordering the alleyway. Mrs. Hong slowed the car, and we greeted them through the lowered windows. Several of the children had Down's syndrome. I blinked back tears as they stared solemnly back at me.

Jaclyn got more and more excited as we got closer; this did not bode well for our convincing her to leave with us again after the visit. Jaclyn's former teacher, the young woman who had accompanied her to our first meeting, was there to greet us and show us around. Jaclyn propelled us forward by our hands; she could not wait to show us off to her friends. She wanted us to see her old room, and we hurried with her up the outside cement staircase.

The children lived in groups of about twenty. Those who were registered for adoption appeared to be in a separate area of the orphanage; they were the lucky ones in a system that limited adoptions to only 6 percent of the institutionalized children. Of these, only 3 percent were actually adopted. This quota system ensured that the rest of the world was not flooded with abandoned Chinese children and allowed the Chinese to "save face" about the severity of the problem caused by their strict population control. Jaclyn had lived with the group of kids that were not registered. Since both she and Jin Xun Li had been involved in adoptions that had fallen through, they had been classified as "unadoptable." The kids in her group ranged in age from about two to eight or nine. When we arrived, they were having what was called "amusement time." They were huddled in a tiny dark room watching a snowy TV screen while seated on hard wooden benches and broken chairs around the perimeter of the room. Upon hearing Jaclyn's shouts, most of the kids came tumbling out into the hall to greet her. A few, however, could not bear to see her excitement. They remained behind in the dank room, sitting passively while silent tears rolled down their cheeks. After seeing this room, I understood better why Jaclyn had recoiled from watching TV in the hotel room.

Jaclyn frantically pushed through the throng of excited children in the hall to find the tiniest child in the back of the TV room. I recognized Xiao Mei Mei immediately from the pictures. He sat listlessly until his eyes lit on Jaclyn. She bent to hold him gently, then stepped back to carefully survey his appearance. She straightened his collar even though it was lying just fine. Bone-thin legs poked out from his sweatpants; Jaclyn carefully pulled the pant legs down over his ankles. Satisfied that he was now dressed properly, she took his hand and he silently accompanied her everywhere. It was amazing to watch. Her attention to him, her gestures, her looks of devotion all seemed uncannily motherlike and uncomfortably out of place for her age.

As if she somehow sensed her special connection to us, Jin Xun Li came running, all smiles, and gave me an exuberant hug. I held her close. She giggled and talked animatedly to me in Chinese, pointing with excitement to the pin I wore with Jaclyn's picture on it. This child was enchanting; clearly, she was the life of the party. She ran to Jaclyn and cajoled her into doing a song-and-dance number with her. Finally, after the teacher prodded her, too, she did. The two girls stood side by side, singing in Chinese and performing an elaborate dance. Jaclyn looked sullen during this command performance. In contrast, Jin Xun Li gave it her all. After they finished, to our enthusiastic applause, Jin Xun Li tried to convince Jaclyn to do another number. Jaclyn sullenly refused and moved away. This did not dampen Jin Xun Li's enthusiasm at all; she simply began to sing and dance on her own. She was desperate for attention; it was as if she were auditioning for parents. The other children vied for our attention, too, but none with the charm, verve, and moxie of Jin Xun Li. I noticed how markedly different in appearance she and Jaclyn were from the other children. They both seemed much sturdier. It made me wonder if those who were to be adopted were given more food, as had been the practice at Christy's orphanage.

The children clung to us, examining everything, touching us desperately. They were delighted by the fact that Jaclyn and I wore matching navy flowered jumpers. I had selected these outfits intentionally to convey to her that she and I belonged together; this message was not lost on the other children either.

Jaclyn, with Xiao Mei Mei firmly gripping her hand while walking beside her, proudly showed us her bed. The room was so crammed with beds it was nearly impossible to navigate the space. It was a large room with a single window; all twenty children slept here. The beds were high off the ground and solidly constructed of wood. They were very small, and each held a tiny pillow and a comforter. The walls, once painted with cheerful cartoon characters, were badly peeling. Mildew and water stains streaked the ceiling and walls.

The children told Jaclyn that they had not been fed that day since breakfast. And from the waiflike appearance of most of them, this was most likely not unusual. Jaclyn, clearly a leader in the group, boldly confronted the teacher about this on behalf of her friends. With obvious embarrassment the teacher explained that they had run out of food. The older kids had been skipped so the younger ones could eat. With all the confidence of one who had now had a mother for three entire days, Jaclyn told her friends, "Don't worry. I'll ask my mom to give you something to eat." With that, twenty hungry faces turned to look at me, unsure whether to believe the boast of my new daughter. If I had only known; I never felt so inadequate in all my life. I dug to the bottom of my purse but produced nothing. Jaclyn then handed over the one hard candy she was holding to the oldest boy, a child of about nine, who carefully divided it with his teeth so that each of the twenty children could have a sliver. I knew that the memory of that raw need would haunt me forever. I wondered how God looked down upon these children without weeping.

Although Jaclyn told the kids that her parents had brought them things, I had foolishly forgotten the bag of toys I had packed for the orphanage, and we had surrendered our gifts of clothes to the assistant director when we arrived. Jaclyn was incensed, demanding to know from the staff where the things were that her parents had brought. She seemed especially upset that she could not give any clothes to Xiao Mei Mei. I didn't understand her behavior; it was as if she did not trust the adults there to make sure her friends got the new clothes. As I looked around at the stark reality of the sparse institution, our bags of donations seemed like very little in comparison to the needs there, only a drop in the bucket.

Nevertheless, Jaclyn chatted animatedly with her friends. She told them that she now had parents and lots of new clothes and toys. Although we were happy, and more than a little surprised, to see how pleased she seemed, the effect of her exuberant joy was that the other children slowly became more despondent. Several of them already looked nearly lifeless. They walked with slow shuffles as if even the effort required to lift their feet was too much for them. Their eyes looked at us flatly; they had no expectations. The teacher saw their sadness and, anxious for the source of it to leave, began to hurry us along.

As we prepared to go, Xiao Mei Mei began to cry in a way that I had never seen before. He was entirely still, making no sound at all, as tears streamed down his cheeks. Jaclyn picked him up and began to comfort him. Although he was barely a head shorter than she was, she lifted him capably. She spoke to him soothingly in a gentle singsong voice, urging him not to cry. She rocked him gently as if he were a baby. She lovingly caressed his cheek as the teacher reminded her that it was time for her to leave. He stood alone, silent and bereft, as she stoically waved good-bye. It was excruciatingly painful to watch.

But nothing compared to hearing Jin Xun Li wail, "I wish I had a mom and a dad, too!" and the choking, heart-wrenching sobbing that followed. There are no words big enough to describe this pain. Watching it, I knew that this is what it feels like when your heart breaks; I didn't know if mine would ever be whole again.

I turned back to comfort her, unsure of what to do, and desperately hoped that the teacher or another adult would go to her and hold her. Instead, this display of grief made the teacher even more anxious to remove us. I turned one last time and watched the solitary figure of this little girl, body pressed against the railing, crying so hard that she could barely catch her breath. The sound of her sobbing echoed against the concrete walls of the institution and could be heard until we got outside. My eyes were so full of tears that I could hardly see to put one foot in front of the other. My gut instinct was to run back and grab as many of the children as I could and take them out of there. How would I ever be able to forget those forlorn faces? How can there be a world like this on the same earth as the comfortable, safe place that I call home? I knew in an instant that I would never be the same again; this was a life-altering experience. I looked over and saw that Rick, Emily, and even our driver were choking back tears. But even though every fiber of my being told me to turn back, we continued to walk away.

As we made our way downstairs, we passed room after room filled with children. The nurseries contained row upon row of light blue cribs, so many that we couldn't count them. Some of the older babies stood in their cribs peering at us; they were incredibly beautiful. I think the saddest part, though, was the areas of the institution where the disabled children were sequestered. The signs above the doors, written in both Chinese and English, labeled these children "the deformed." Workers picked some of them up so they could peer at us through the open windows. A beautiful child marred by a serious cleft lip smiled sweetly at us. Several children who were unable to ambulate crawled pitifully across the floor.

We were thrilled to discover that the director had modified her schedule to accommodate us, and we were taken to her office to wait for her. While we waited, we asked the teacher for some general information about Jaclyn's health and background. Little was shared with us. I asked about the multiple scars on her face. Somewhat defensively, she answered that Jaclyn had arrived there with these scars. It was subtly suggested that her parents had abused her. I was appalled at how matter-of-factly this painful information was given in Jaclyn's presence. She, however, seemed unfazed by the discussion. We had been told in advance some sketchy facts about her abandonment. She had been left in a forest, presumably to die, but was instead discovered and taken to a police station. The police in turn had brought her here. Her age had been estimated as two and a half years old. Abandonment was unusual for this province. The orphanage was well known and active in the adoption program; it was hard to understand why her birth mother had not abandoned her here, under cover of darkness, as Chinese law limiting family size had forced so many others to do. But this sad story, which had wreaked havoc upon my soul for so long, was not markedly different from the tragedies that had led to the arrival of any of Jaclyn's peers.

Her teacher asked Jaclyn how she liked her new parents. Emily's interpretation of her answer was that we were "OK." Actually, given how the week had gone, we were thrilled with this judgment; it was better than we dared hope. Jaclyn did have a complaint to register, however. "My parents are foreigners," she told her teacher with the manner of one who had been awarded second best. The adults all chuckled over her clear disappointment on this score. She did brag, however, that she was now getting milk and good food to eat.

Then the director entered. A tall, slim woman around forty years old with long hair neatly coiled, she greeted us with effortless grace. I immediately had the sense that I was in the presence of greatness. An aura of kindness radiated from her. I thought that this was what it must feel like to be in the presence of someone like Mother Teresa; I suddenly felt very small and unworthy.

She sat on a small rattan sofa facing us and talked directly to us. Even though Emily was translating for both sides, and I suspect doing a *Reader's Digest* version of it, it was as if we could understand her. I was drawn to her sincerity and genuine warmth. She started by saying, "Thank you for adopting Lou Jiao," while clasping our hands warmly between both of hers. "My happiest days are when adoptive parents come. I tell the children that these are the most important parents because they will be with you for your whole life. You came at a time when she needs you so."

Rick tried to thank her for the important work she was doing, but she quickly brushed aside our thanks. "This is not my work," she said simply. "It is my life. It is my joy. I instead admire you for the good deed you have done. Although we try very hard to provide good care, it does not compare to having a family, to having parents.

"I also admire those in Gualing that invite the children to their homes for special holidays. Unfortunately," she added with apparent sadness, "Lou Jiao has never been chosen to go."

She touched briefly on the sketchy facts of Lou Jiao's abandonment, providing us with no more information than we already had other than this tidbit, which we completely misunderstood: "The policeman who brought her here told us her name." Sometimes conversation loses important elements in the translation; we wrongly assumed from this anecdote that he had chosen her name.

"Even though I see so much that is sad," she continued, "I was heartbroken about the way that Lou Jiao was discarded." I glanced at Jaclyn in alarm as this was spoken; she did not recoil at this harsh word as I did. "For this reason," the director continued, "I personally chose her birthday. For a child with such a sad beginning I wanted her to have the luckiest birth date I could think of." She had chosen October 1, the anniversary of the Communist takeover of China and a day of national celebration there. All of China would celebrate her special day.

We asked her what words she wanted to leave with Lou Jiao, what hopes she had for her future. On this topic she was passionate. "My wish for her future is that she will grow up to help other people. That she will know that caring for others is the most important purpose in life. Actually, that it is the only true purpose, the only real legacy."

And then she looked at us solemnly and said, "Please make sure that Lou Jiao grows up to be a caring person and to be responsible. This is so important; that a person is responsible both to their family and to society. This orphanage exists because of the lack of responsibility on the part of parents. I want these children to do better with their own lives." We promised her that we, too, shared this belief and would instill it in our child. We talked with her for at least an hour. It was, without a doubt, the most powerful conversation of my life. Rick and I were both in tears as we left.

As we made our final descent down the cement staircase, Jaclyn exuberantly blew kisses to all the assembled staff, who lined the staircase to wish her well. Like the children, the staff were teary-eyed. She said a special good-bye to an elderly man whose job it was to man the front gate; he was the one who each morning brought in the new arrivals that had been left there by desperate mothers during the night. Even he threw kisses back to her. She really seemed fine. By contrast, we were emotional wrecks.

As the car pulled away, I desperately wished that there was a way to know with certainty the fates of all we left behind and especially the precious Jin Xun Li. Or maybe they were fates best left unknown.

As we drove away, I was lost in thought. What I finally began to realize was that to know Jaclyn was to see the embodiment of hope. Through this small glimpse of her life inside the orphanage, I could see that this radiant little soul had not allowed the darkness of her situation to diminish her life-affirming hopefulness. As I was beginning to see glimpses of who Jaclyn really was, I better understood the tears that were shed as she left the orphanage. I knew that some of the other children's sadness was over the loss of this bright light in their lives; I was sure that the darkness there had become even thicker with Jaclyn gone.

By contrast, in many ways my own life was becoming brighter. Jaclyn turned to me, and out of the clear blue fiercely proclaimed, "I lubba you. I LUBBA YOU!"

I love you too, kid.

Chapter Four

Finding Her Way Home

A part of us remains wherever we have been.
—Unknown

As our final days in China drew to a close, we realized that we would soon lose the ability to communicate with Jaclyn. She was just beginning to talk openly with Emily, and what she had to say was fascinating. She was remarkably verbal, and everyone was surprised by how well she expressed herself.

Jaclyn told Emily that she was very upset with Jin Xun Li for her behavior at the orphanage. She thought that Jin Xun Li was showing off because she, too, wanted to go with Jaclyn's new parents. We later learned that Jaclyn had helped take care of Jin Xun Li when she was younger; the girls are about a year apart in age. This added to Jaclyn's resentment of her behavior. It was as if she was saying, "Hey, I gave that kid the best years of my life and this is how she thanks me?"

After Jin Xun Li had reached the age of independence, about two and a half years old, Jaclyn told Emily that her new "job" at the orphanage was to take care of Xiao Mei Mei and a toddler girl she called Po Po. This must be the reason why these younger children were in her group. She said they slept in the bed next to hers, and she got them up, washed them, and dressed them. The photos from the orphanage supported this; she was shown dressing herself in one photo and dressing the children in the next bed in another. She said she sheltered them from the big kids and comforted them when they cried or were sad. I wondered if this was the reason why she called out Xiao Mei Mei's name each night when she was falling asleep. I guessed that it explained what we had seen—how she ran to this child, adjusting his clothes, holding him, and cradling him like a baby. She had acted like a little mother. I was shocked and disbelieving; how could a child not yet four years old have such responsibility? Surely there was not a world, even here, where children mothered children? But, sadly, there was no disputing the veracity of her words.

As the days passed, much of Jaclyn's conversation was about Xiao

Mei Mei; she relished telling anecdotes about him. On her third day as our daughter she had begun a less than subtle campaign to have "mama's family" adopt Xiao Mei Mei. What I didn't know then was that it would continue every day from that day forward.

She told us over and over, all day long, what a good boy he was and how much he needed a mama and a home. This was my first inkling that to know Jaclyn would be to understand something new about love. I already understood the healing power of love; I had seen how it restored life and spirit to my Chinese baby, Christy. But Jaclyn showed me a different kind of love. She told us, "Big girls like me can take care of ourselves. So we need to help the little ones." She told us that she took good care of Po Po but that she gave all her love to Xiao Mei Mei. What I began to realize was that in a world many imagine as loveless, a world without mothers, Jaclyn knew how to give selfless mother love. Even when she had none herself. And this was how she first showed love to me. She was so grateful for my loving care that she wanted to love me in the only way she knew how—by brushing my hair, covering me up, giving me her doll to sleep with. When I had thought of all the challenges inherent in an older child adoption, I had never imagined I would have to teach Jaclyn how to be a child.

Too soon it was time to go home. We hugged and kissed our travel mates good-bye, vowing to keep in touch, and headed off to the Beijing airport for the long flight home. The airport was mobbed with Chinese citizens, and the line at the border patrol, where passports were carefully scrutinized, was unmoving. In fact, as is typical in China, there was no actual line but rather a mob of people pushing forward through a narrow passage. It was impossible to move and nearly impossible to breathe. From Jaclyn's vantage point it must have seemed like a terrifying sea of legs, but she came with us willingly, and I gave little thought to what she might be feeling. In truth, she had no choice. She had no voice. She had no idea what awaited her. Because she was compliant, I was not concerned. But I did not know her well enough then to read the look in her eyes. Now when I look back at pictures of that day, I can see it clearly. The fear. The confusion. The pain. The utter terror. It was all there.

After two hours in a logjam of humanity, we were released to leave the country. Jaclyn's passport had been accepted without question, and we hurried down the hallway to our flight. I stared out the airplane window and blinked away tears as the last sights of China faded from view. The mountains. The vistas. The lush green valleys. The rivers. Jaclyn's homeland. It would soon be gone.

I knew what awaited me on the other end of this thirteen-hour flight: my home. My mother and father, Nana and Pops to my children, who still lived in my childhood home just a few minutes from my house. My sister Willow, who had generously helped with my children while I was gone. Laura and Jeff, who would soon be off to China themselves to adopt a yet-unknown daughter. And my girls. How I longed to hold them. My precious Kate, the one who had so willingly accepted the thought of another new sister and who I knew waited joyfully to welcome Jaclyn to our family. And my baby, Christy. My arms ached to hold her. Her second birthday had passed while we were in China. She had no understanding of time. She must think we had abandoned her. How would she feel now about sharing me with this new sister? I thought of our family, as it had been prior to this trip, as a tapestry, the colors blended wondrously together, the handiwork smooth and perfect. Our family dynamic had been so right; would it now be as if I had ripped a hole in the center and was trying to patch it with a new swatch of fabric that somehow didn't fit? Or would the threads once again run seamlessly together so that it would never be apparent to those viewing it that the tapestry had been reworked?

Rick had his own thoughts about our new addition. Having already seen ample evidence of Jaclyn's strong personality and how she was clearly a ringleader in her group, Rick joked that the staff at the orphanage had probably run around giving each other high fives after we left with her. But I remembered clearly the love in their eyes and the tears that they tried hard not to show. I knew it would be impossible to know this child and not to care for her; I was certain that young and old alike missed her desperately.

But I still was not seeing her through the rose-colored glasses of mother love. Instead, I saw her objectively. I saw her love and compassion and gentleness. But I also saw how hurtful she could be; how she secretly gloated when she rejected Rick's efforts to hold her hand, how she relished my pain when she refused to sit by me and chose Emily instead. I had seen her delight and her wonder, but I had also seen her boldness and her defiance. I had seen her joy, but I had also seen her pain and rage. And these were emotions almost fearsome to behold. She was still a puzzle to me. How long would it be before she seemed familiar, like my own child; until I could love her like Kate, the one who had grown under my heart, and Christy, the one who had grown in it?

The empty place inside me that had longed for her for so long was finally full; in fact, it was overflowing. But I could not shake the nagging fear that the life I had known, one that was calm, predictable, safe, and manageable, was now over. And in its place was something unknown.

But once again, in stark contrast to my fear, I saw Jaclyn's stalwart bravery. She sat stoically, having no idea, beyond the pictures she had been shown, of the world that lay ahead of her. A world of people who all looked different, who sounded different, who were different. Unimaginable sights and sounds. A home that she was now expected to call her own. A family of strangers she would be expected to embrace. Everything that was familiar to her had been ripped away. And I realized once again what a huge sacrifice this child had been asked to make when I held out my hand to her.

Chapter Five

To Know Jaclyn

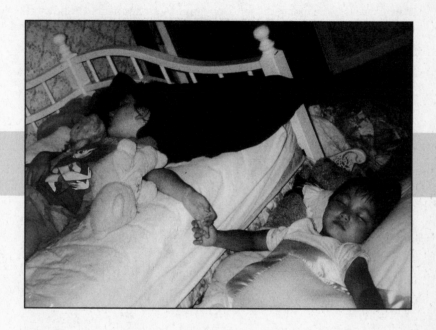

It is a very simple secret: It is only with the heart that one can see rightly.
—Antoine de Saint-Exupéry

The plane landed and we hurried in our zombielike, sleep-deprived state through the customs and immigration processes. I could hardly wait for the first glimpse of my family and the chance to show off our newest member. Our family waved balloons and "Welcome Home" banners and held out their arms in excitement when they glimpsed us behind our mountain of luggage.

I had dressed Jaclyn and myself in our matching mother-daughter jumpers and had requested that my sister Willow dress Kate and Christy in their matching jumpers, too. I felt like a reject from *The Sound of Music* but hoped it would help Jaclyn identify who her new sisters were and understand that we were all one family unit. My baby, Christy, ran into my outstretched arms, while Jaclyn wrapped herself tightly around Rick, using both arms and legs, and buried her head in his shoulder. Our friends and family allowed her space. Kate was the exception. As soon as Rick put Jaclyn down, Kate approached her and gently embraced her, putting her arm protectively around her shoulders. Jaclyn stood stiffly, head down, and barely raised her eyes to give Kate a curious glance. Kate's gesture was so like her; her heart was filled with love and acceptance. She desperately wanted to love Jaclyn.

Once we arrived home, Jaclyn raced in open-mouthed wonder through our condominium. She gasped in delight at the large dollhouse and stood openmouthed staring at all the toys. But it wasn't long before the sibling dynamics began in earnest. Jaclyn hugged Christy too hard in a choking neck hold. Christy immediately retaliated by bopping Jaclyn on the head. I rushed in to break it up, this the first physical fight ever under my roof, but my intervention wasn't necessary. Christy had asserted herself by establishing her boundaries, and the two of them rarely had issues again. Over time they would prove to be truly sisters; in headlocks shoving like sumo wrestlers one minute and cuddling in bed watching a favorite show the next. But Jaclyn had a natural affinity for little ones, a gentleness that belied her years.

Kate had a much harder time adjusting to Jaclyn. Even early on, I began to despair that they would ever find their rhythm. Jaclyn seemed to delight in grabbing things from Kate and teasing her; suddenly the concept of sharing seemed foreign to her. She seemed to see older children as natural predators and feel that to protect herself, she had to strike the first blow. Kate would come to me crying several times a day over Jaclyn's teasing. But Kate was unfailingly kind in return. To strike back, to assert herself, was not in her gentle nature. And Jaclyn, sensing weakness, steamrollered over her every chance she had. She cheated at games. She stole Kate's prized possessions and refused to give them back. She would assume a fierce stance, fists raised menacingly as if for battle, and Kate would run from her shrieking in terror.

"Why is Jaclyn so mean to me, Mama?" Kate would ask through tears of frustration. I tried to explain about the survival-of-the-fittest environment that Jaclyn had come from and how it had caused her to fear those larger than herself, but Kate could not understand; that world was too remote to be fathomable to a child who had never known want. Instead, Kate tried everything to win Jaclyn over. Kate ate with chopsticks; Jaclyn insisted on eating with a fork. Kate tried to play according to Jaclyn's desires until her teasing finally wore her down and she would retreat, seeking solace from me.

I learned early on that it was fruitless to expect Jaclyn to apologize for any of her bad behavior as I expected my other children to do. Jaclyn would have sat in the time-out chair for days before she proffered an apology. I was angered by her stubborn refusal to offer this simple act of contrition. I joined a group of moms who had adopted older children from China; it was a support group that I desperately needed. One of the things I discovered through my conversations with others in the group was that Jaclyn's behavior reflected a cultural norm: to "lose face" was much worse than to accept punishment. Her past, still a puzzle to me, had made her who she was, and I knew that I needed to understand that better to really know how to parent her.

At bedtime, still another child would emerge, one entirely different from the fierce and resilient child I saw all day long. No matter how mean she had been during the day, Jaclyn could not fall asleep without Kate holding her hand. And Kate, sensing how terrified Jaclyn was of the dark, would comply without question even though the different heights of the beds meant that she had to sleep with her arm hanging uncomfortably downward.

Jaclyn had fought sleep since she'd been with us, and I believed it was because this was when the demons came out, when all her fears rose to the surface.

As we climbed the stairs one evening, Jaclyn was noticeably agitated over the fact that Rick was not home. He had an evening meeting to attend and would not be home until much later. Her security was still so fragile that she could not stand the absence of even one member of her new family. Oftentimes after I put her to bed she would call downstairs, "Mama?" at five minute intervals to reassure herself that I was still there. This was sometimes followed by "Don't go!" an almost whispered plea.

Once I had made the mistake of going down to the basement to have a private phone call with a friend. Jaclyn had called me over and over and, getting no response, had climbed from her bed and searched the house. Still not able to locate me, she had raced out into the front yard, screaming my name over and over until she fell to her knees, her arms raised skyward and screamed, "MAMA! MAMA!" at the heavens. I found her there, in a frenzied state that took hours to calm, and wondered what our neighbors thought.

She did not want to go to sleep without Rick, so she dragged out her bedtime routine, performing each task with mind-numbing slowness. She undressed at a snail's pace. She took eons of time to get her Barbie nightgown on. Kate was nearly asleep by the time she had brushed her teeth. She was always careful of her possessions. Unlike my other two who promptly threw their dirty clothes in a crumpled heap on the floor, Jaclyn would fold her still-clean clothes with precision, smoothing each crease and carefully tucking them away in her drawers. She did all this with meticulous slowness while I nearly curled up in the bed myself from exhaustion, prodding her on but knowing it would do no good.

But my annoyance with her dissipated as I watched her tuck her own teddy bear in with Christy as she gently stroked Christy's hand and bade her good night. "This like I do with Xiao Mei Mei," she said when she saw me watching her. "But he not have little bear." At night she always spoke of him, often calling out his name as she drifted off to sleep. "I hold Xiao Mei Mei's hand when he go night so he not scared," she said. I knew he was not the only one who was afraid.

I lay down next to Jaclyn in her trundle bed, and she began to gently stroke my face. "So pur-dee, Mama," she said while she looked lovingly into my eyes. How could I resist that? Then, when I got ready to leave, she said in agitation what had been her first full sentence in English: "Don't *touch* it! Don't SHUT THE DOOR!"

My hand was nowhere near the door, but I stopped in surprise at the near hysteria in her tone. I seized this opportunity to negotiate with the child who would now launch into at least an hour of songs and fits of giggles until her sister, irritated by her wakefulness, would call out to me in annoyance to make her stop.

"I'll leave the door open if you will be quiet and go to sleep," I said. It was a bluff. I knew she needed the nightlight on, the door fully open, the hall light blazing in her eyes, and the bathroom light on to even attempt sleep.

"OK," Jaclyn replied and then, "Give me high five!"

I did and we sealed the deal.

But Jaclyn willed herself to stay awake until Rick got home, and hours later when she heard his key in the lock she called down to him, "Daddy! Daddy!"

"Why are you still awake, Jaclyn?" Rick chided gently. "It's very late."

"Xiao Mei Mei scared 'cause no Jack-win," she said sadly. Rick, like me, could hardly bear to hear these endless reminders of her loss. He tried to change the subject by talking to her briefly about the events of the day, and then he kissed her gently. As he started to leave the room, Jaclyn called out, "I lubba you, Daddy!" It was the first time she had initiated this sentiment, and Rick was nearly in tears when he told me about it.

"I've never heard sweeter words," he said. "Maybe because they were so long in coming. I had to earn them!"

Yes, Jaclyn did not open her heart easily; it had been broken too many times. She saved her love for those she knew she could count on not to disappoint her in return. How privileged I felt to be one of them.

I spent what seemed like days doing laundry, while the dire predictions of those who already had three children rang in my head: expect incredible amounts of wash, everywhere you decide to go will be a big production, expect a dizzying amount of activity. It was already apparent that these warnings were coming true.

But none of them captured the most significant change in our household, which was simply the amount of laughter. Jaclyn would set the girls into fits of giggling with her silly antics. She would show up out of the clear blue wearing tiny doll glasses perched on her nose. She would dance delightedly to any music she heard. She would make Kate and Christy chase her and then pop out of her hiding place laughing uproariously. Sometimes the walls seem to actually reverberate with the giggles of the three little girls.

Because to know Jaclyn was to know joy. This was a child who embraced life. She ran down the stairs each morning with a smile on her face and hugged me exuberantly. She could hardly wait to see what each day had in store for her, which amazed me, given where she had been. She had a giggle that was contagious and belly-laughed when she teased us with her unabashed sense of humor.

But I soon began to realize that to know Jaclyn was also to know sorrow. Sometimes, when it was dark, all the feelings that she could not express overwhelmed her. As wave after wave of grief, homesickness, fear, pain, and other feelings too strong for words washed over her, she would cling to my neck as if she were drowning. I would retreat to the rocking chair in the girls' room and rock her for what seemed to be hours. When she was in these depths, it seemed as if she could not hear my words of comfort. But somehow she found her way out of these murky waters, gulping for air, grasping for safe ground again.

Shortly after arriving home, we headed out to a pool party my mother had planned for the Fourth of July weekend. My mother's sister, Jaclyn's namesake, would be there with her family, and I was anxious for everyone to meet our new daughter. Jaclyn was shy with a yard full of strangers and had a detached, almost sick look on her face when I insisted that she pose for a picture with my aunt Jackie. But it didn't take her long to become intrigued by the pool, and, showing her natural exuberance for new things, she was soon playing excitedly with Kate and Christy in the water. It was a perfect day for swimming—hot and sunny—so the adults made their way into the pool, too. Jeff and Laura were there with their four-year-old daughter, Kirsten, and two-year-old Elise. Both girls were shy and timid, as Laura had been as a child, and chose instead to sit on the edge of the pool, dangling their feet in the water. Since his own daughters were choosing to sit things out, Jeff approached Jaclyn, who took an immediate shine to him, and got her to play in the water with him. Jaclyn delighted in his attention and soon was shrieking in joy as he spun her through the water. Jeff was taken with her spirit, her exuberance, and her lack of fear in this, another new experience for her. Before long he had persuaded her to climb to the top of the eight-foot water slide and ride down into the pool with him. After a few turns, Jaclyn was sliding alone as he stood at the bottom waiting to catch her.

The adults feasted on a huge picnic spread—potato salad, steak, watermelon, and desserts of every kind—while we wondered among ourselves what Jaclyn was thinking as she so quickly embraced this new world. Then, on her umpteenth time down the slide, Jaclyn's tiny foot slipped on the wet step, and she fell about six feet. Although I ran to catch her, it was too late. She hit the cement deck with a sickening thud, scraping her cheek on the rough surface as her groin landed on the protruding metal plumbing. She came to me sobbing, and I held her wet form tightly against me, trying to comfort her. My mother, a registered nurse, checked her carefully for broken bones. Seeing none, she retreated, while I tried to check the source of bleeding in Jaclyn's groin. She had her legs pulled up too tightly against her body for me to see it clearly, but I assumed it was nothing serious. There was little blood, she was not screaming in pain, and I didn't want to seem like a hysterical mother. The other adults were dismayed and worried. She had enjoyed herself so much; would this cause her to be frightened of the pool?

Finally her crying slowed, and Rick examined the wound area more closely. Once I got a good glimpse of it, I gasped. The cut was deep and more than two inches long; it would need several stitches. Rick picked her up as I rushed behind them to the car, calling out over my shoulder to my mother to please keep Kate and Christy for me. She assured me she would; while my father, sick with guilt over the incident, busied himself trying to figure out how this freak accident had occurred.

The emergency room was nearly deserted, as it was a holiday; the only other waiting patient was an elderly Asian man. Jaclyn's eyes filled with fear as she looked around the medical facility. There was no pediatrician available, and a young resident came to examine her. Clearly inexperienced with children, he was unsure how to proceed and was anxious to calm her fear. I then remembered the Asian man I had seen in the waiting room; perhaps he spoke Chinese?

He was found and did indeed speak Mandarin. Although we were not sure what, if anything, Jaclyn could understand, he began slowly translating the physician's words for her, explaining what would happen next. She listened intently to him but could not choke down her fear. She cried inconsolably while they gave her shots to numb the area, and she screamed in horror when the suturing began.

I laid my body, still clad only in my swimsuit, across the gurney, nearly on it, in an attempt to reassure her. I held her hand and tried to make it all seem less frightening. At first I was not even aware of the tears that streamed down my own face. Then, after a time, the only one crying harder than Jaclyn was I. I felt like an inept mother because I could not put up a brave front for her. But I couldn't stop the tears. I cried for her fear in the face of all the strangeness. I cried because I didn't know the right words to comfort her, words she could understand. I cried because I couldn't understand her words. I cried over the unfairness of this terrible accident marring her joyous day. I cried over the unfairness of all the childhood pleasures that had been denied her. We cried together, and I felt ashamed that I was not holding it together better for her. And then when we had both stopped crying, I realized that in this instant, everything had changed. I realized that my tears were because I loved her. Her pain was my pain. Her fear was my fear. She was my child. I loved her fiercely. I was not lying anymore when I said those words. I loved her like a mother. And the sure knowledge of this truth made my tears start again. For better or for worse, from this day on, she was my own child.

Chapter Six

Jaclyn's New Life

To be a star you must follow your own light, follow your own path, and never fear the darkness, for that is when the stars shine the brightest.
—Unknown

Too soon, *I needed to return to* work. To alleviate my guilt, I convinced myself that Jaclyn would feel at home at the Montessori school that Kate attended. After all, Jaclyn was used to being in a structured environment with children all day; being in a family was what was still unfamiliar to her.

As we drove up to the school on the first day, I desperately wished for words to communicate with her about this strange new place. I worried that she would fear abandonment. "Mama will come back, Jaclyn," I said to her in a soothing voice. "Mama will *always* come back." She looked at me stoically, her eyes unblinking, and marched inside the school with Kate at her side.

Kate's best friend at school was a kindred spirit named Olivia, who was one year younger. Olivia was a loving and gentle little girl, and she and Kate were inseparable. Kate put a gentle arm around her sister and took her over to introduce her to Olivia.

"This is my new sister, Jaclyn. She's from China," Kate said solemnly. "Will you be her friend now too, OK?" Olivia nodded her assent, and from that moment forward the former twosome became a threesome. Jaclyn had trouble pronouncing Olivia's name and called her "I-lovea-you" instead; it was a fitting moniker for this very loving little girl. At the end of her first day of school, the teacher told me that Kate had gently guided Jaclyn through the day's activities and was a continual comforting presence at her side. I wasn't at all surprised.

I marveled at the way Kate had willingly, unhesitatingly opened her heart to two siblings in one and a half years. She had given up her room without a moment's hesitation. She was unfailingly kind to both of her sisters. I knew that my past successes with Kate were what had made me arrogant enough to think I knew something about parenting. Without that confidence, I would never have been able to add two more children with a multitude of needs. And, if truth were told, if Kate's whole heart had not been in it, too, I would not have been able to do it. It's as if Kate always knew, in her six-year-old heart, that a family was formed by something other than biology.

Jaclyn's English developed very rapidly. She spoke in full sentences, conveying fairly complex thoughts, within weeks. I found that there were many colloquial expressions that were puzzling to her and, as with all children, expressions that she did not understand. She questioned relentlessly, unwilling to give up until she had a complete understanding of what was being explained. Jaclyn wouldn't let something that confused her drop, even if it was beyond her comprehension.

A few weeks after we had come home, I took the girls to a local playground on a warm Saturday. Jaclyn began to play close by a small boy who was industriously digging a very deep hole in the sandbox. The boy was there with his grandparents, who began to gently tease him about digging "all the way to China." I saw Jaclyn perk up at the first mention of the word *China*.

Jaclyn moved closer to the family and began to eavesdrop on their conversation. As they continued to joke about the hole "all the way to China," I watched Jaclyn size them up, as if to say, "Hmmm . . . grandparents usually know what they are talking about." Then, finally, she couldn't stand it anymore. She gently nudged the little boy aside and, with hope written all over her face, stuck her head into the hole. Her eyes were filled with disappointment when she looked up. She came over to me, her head bowed, and sat down dejectedly.

"No China," she said. I guess when the road traveled had been so long, it was hard not to wish for a shortcut.

Over the next few weeks, I made appointments for Jaclyn with the pediatrician and the dentist. Again I was at a loss to explain to her what would happen at these strange new places. I was filled with pangs of guilt when she excitedly bounded into the dentist's office with a smile of anticipation, but she stoically endured the dental work needed to repair years of decay. Then she received all her required vaccinations at the pediatrician's office. Often tears would fill her eyes, but she would resolutely blink them back. I thought these unpleasant experiences would dim her enthusiasm and maybe even her trust in me, but every time I asked her to get into the car, even though the destination was unknown to her, she climbed in as if great adventure awaited her.

And most of the time, great adventure did await her. Everyday events were transformed when I saw Jaclyn's reaction to them. We took the girls to the Michigan State Fair in August. Jaclyn delighted in the farm animals, listening carefully as I explained what each animal was. As we entered the horse stables, Christy, frightened by the intimidating size of the animals, began to cry.

"It OK, baby," Jaclyn said soothingly, kneeling by her stroller. "Jack-win here. Big hor-see not get you." Then, as if to reassure me about Christy's reaction, she added, "Xiao Mei Mei be scared of big hor-see." I wasn't surprised at all by this remark; I was now used to Xiao Mei Mei always walking beside us. As we left the barn, Jaclyn said to me in a stage whisper, "Horse PON-NEE [potty] STANK-EE!"

When the State Fair parade rounded the corner, Jaclyn ran forward, pushing her way through the crowd to secure a front row view. She marched in place in imitation of the bands, savoring the loud music. We looked for a spot to sit and rest and eat our snacks, but all the picnic tables were filled. We settled down on the grass to eat, while Jaclyn watched us with disdain.

"Sit down, Jaclyn," I said, patting the spot next to me.

"I not get all dirty," she said as she remained standing. Rick chuckled at her fastidiousness given that she had lived in near squalor just a few weeks earlier.

Kate encouraged Jaclyn to come with her on the kiddie rides, and with the security of having her big sister at her side, Jaclyn was game. Before long she was laughing out loud on the rides and running with Kate to get in line for the next one. I could hardly believe that this was the same child who had shrieked in terror at the amusement park rides we saw in China. There, when we had instructed Emily to ask Jaclyn if she wanted to go on a ride, Jaclyn's response had been: "I'd rather play with Xiao Mei Mei. I just want to play with Xiao Mei Mei." Even then he had walked everywhere with us.

At the end of the day, Rick surprised the girls with heaping ice cream cones. Jaclyn repeated "Thank-a you, Daddy, for ice cream" over and over as we headed back to the car.

"Thank-a you, Mama, for big fun," she said to me, her arms opened expansively as we got in the car. Before I could even begin to savor her gratefulness, she looked into my eyes and added: "You be Xiao Mei Mei's mama so he get ice cream and see big music, too? *Penache* [please]? *Penache?*"

"Get into your car seat, Jaclyn," I said wearily as I tried to shake off the heavy shroud of guilt that now snuffed out some of the joy of the day.

At the end of August, Kate had to leave the Montessori school to start first grade at the local public school. I was worried about how Jaclyn, who had come to rely on her so much, would adjust to being on her own. I didn't know that Kate had the issue covered.

"Olivia," Kate said solemnly on her last day at the Montessori school, "you have to promise to be Jaclyn's best friend after I'm gone. You have to help her, because she doesn't understand everything yet. You have to take care of Jaclyn and watch out for her. Don't let the other kids tease her." Olivia promised and proved over time to be true to her word. Although she, too, was often puzzled by Jaclyn's teasing and fierceness, she was loving to Jaclyn in return. She greeted Jaclyn each day with a big hug. She used her allowance to buy Jaclyn a special necklace. She always saved the seat next to her for Jaclyn.

As the parents watched me come and go from school each day with my three little ducklings in tow, they became bolder in their questioning about my new addition. Several times I was asked about Jaclyn and Christy, "Are they sisters?" This question made me smile. My three girls had been sisters from the first minute they glimpsed each other. They fought like sisters, they giggled like sisters, they played like sisters, and they loved like sisters. They could treat each other with horrific meanness but were the first to watch out for each other, too. They slept holding hands. Jaclyn was the first to speak up against any injustice she thought Christy had suffered. They had not a common drop of blood between them but could not have had a stronger bond.

I answered with a resounding "Yes!" And when they clarified their question by saying, "No, I mean are they *real* sisters?" I was truthfully able to say with a smile, "Yes, they are real sisters."

To know Jaclyn was to know gratitude. Over time, her vision of the world transformed my own. One day I picked Jaclyn up early from Montessori school; I needed to get some groceries. As I had yet to pick up Kate from her school and Christy from her sitter's house, I was in a rush. The kids were always hungry for dinner as soon as they entered the door. I scoffed at the recipes for quick thirty-minute dinners; my challenge was to find meals that could be prepared in three minutes or less.

I parked my car haphazardly and grabbed the first cart I could find. Jaclyn was intrigued when I placed her in the seat at the front of the cart, delighted with this new ride. As I despise grocery shopping and was trying to race the clock, I began haphazardly throwing things into my cart. As soon as they landed, Jaclyn squealed with pleasure. She craned around in her seat and snatched each item out of the cart, wanting to hold it, touch it, and revel in it. Then she would turn to me with excitement on her face and ask shyly, "For Jack-win?"

When I nodded yes each time, she would carefully place the item back in the cart and then hold the next. She touched each one as if it were a rare and precious commodity. She nearly shrieked in joy as the cart turned down each new aisle.

I paid for the groceries and pushed the cart doggedly to the car. I lifted her out of the cart and told her to get in the car as I loaded the groceries into the trunk. But she stood riveted to the spot next to me. She watched with eyes as round as saucers as I loaded all the bags into the car. Then, with fierce emotion, she embraced me and said, "Oh, *xie xie* [thank you], Mama!"

Her gratitude made me ashamed. She illuminated what was sorely missing from my own life: simple appreciation of the abundance in it. I would find her opening the refrigerator and freezer and just marveling at all the treasures in them. My own life was so rich; how could I never have noticed it?

And so I, one of the few women in America who despises shopping, now looked forward to our shopping excursions together. Jaclyn had a way of making even the local Target store seem like a palace.

Jaclyn coveted the two demi-undershirts that Kate wore in an imitation of grown-up bras and begged to have them, to which Kate responded, "Look, I had to ask Santa specially for these." Translation: "I'm not sharing my Scooby-Doo faux bra with anyone." I decided that the easiest way to remedy this ongoing battle was to buy Jaclyn some new underwear.

As we wheeled down the aisles of Target, Jaclyn could not contain her excitement. "Look, Mama! So PUR-DEE!" she shrieked at everything from Barbie nightgowns to barrettes. She had a hard time even sitting still in the cart. When I put a cartoon-figured demi-undershirt and panties into the cart she was ecstatic. But to my surprise, Jaclyn insisted that Kate get one, too. In fact, each time I put an item into the cart, she demanded to know whom it was for. If it was for her, Kate had to have an identical item or Jaclyn would put hers back. Even though they fought, at heart Jaclyn was a product of her upbringing. She wanted things to be fair and equitable. This was one of the best lessons that orphanage life had taught her.

She tried to advocate for Christy, too, until I convinced her that babies did not wear this type of underwear. We had protracted negotiations over each item; nothing went into the cart without Jaclyn's scrutiny.

"*Penache*, Mama, for Xiao Mei Mei?" she would ask as she eyed the bright pink Barbie underwear. I knew it was fruitless to begin explaining to her that a boy might not appreciate girls' underwear, and in any event there was no way to send any to him. I shook my head no, and her smile disappeared momentarily, as if she could not enjoy her own good fortune when she knew of his need.

When I pushed the cart over to the aisle where the girls' tights were, Jaclyn was beside herself with joy. She could not believe that she was getting tights, too. They were among her favorite things, and she was in awe of the display—the bright colors, the assorted patterns, the various sizes. She smiled incredulously as I put a few pairs into the cart.

As we walked to the car, she insisted on carrying the bag. "This-a mine. I carry," she said, nearly staggering under its bulk but careful not to let it out of her grasp. She thanked me over and over again on the walk to the car and all through the drive home. The car had barely come to a full stop before Jaclyn jumped out and tore through the house yelling, "SISTER! SISTER!" until she found Kate. She dumped out her cherished bag on the living room floor so that she could show Kate all the treasures she had in it. Kate tried to get caught up in her excitement, but it was only new underwear, after all, and she looked at Jaclyn quizzically as she gushed with enthusiasm. Undaunted by Kate's lukewarm reaction, Jaclyn raced up the stairs to lay out her new underwear for the next day, which happened to be picture day at school.

She wanted to try on a pair right away, and I noticed that the underpants she was already wearing were on backward. As I tried to show her how to switch them around, out fell a piece of candy she had hidden in there. I remembered that she used to do this in China, with favorite possessions. It came from not having any special place of her own to put things—neither a drawer nor a shelf to call her own. Of course, this is less of an issue when a child does not have the opportunity to own anything. Since she'd been with us awhile, I thought she had stopped doing this. When she saw my look of dismay, she hurriedly snatched the treat from my hand and ate it.

The next morning Jaclyn appeared bright and early at my bedside and announced that she was ready for school. All she was wearing was her new underwear. It was clear that she intended to wear nothing else. She refused to put on her dress and was puzzled by my insistence that she do so. After all, what good was fancy new underwear if no one could see it? Kate burst into giggles at the ludicrousness of this, but even Kate's reaction did not persuade Jaclyn. A major meltdown occurred over the unreasonableness of a mom who would let you buy nifty underwear but not allow you to display it to the world.

In hopes of preserving Jaclyn's Chinese, I enrolled her in a local Chinese school that met on Saturdays. I thought she would be thrilled. They had a wonderful program followed by several cultural classes. On the first Saturday, my initial challenge was to convince Miss Jaclyn to modify her ensemble for a public appearance. This was not an easy task. She was wearing a blue bandana on her head, carefully tied in the back with a big rubber band. She had barrettes clipped to the side of it; she never actually wore them in her hair. Over this, she was wearing an old baby bonnet backward. She had on gold lamé slippers and a pink feather boa. And she saw absolutely no reason to change this outfit. A battle of the wills ensued before, with great reluctance, she got into the car wearing a more conservative ensemble.

When we arrived at the school, my next challenge was to complete the proper forms and pay all the tuition fees. The fee schedule was all in Chinese, and I seemed to be the only non-Chinese person there. The enrollment clerk found someone to talk to me who patiently wrote the number out for me so I could fill out my check. We then proceeded to the classroom, where several darling, well-mannered children were sitting politely in their chairs. Their moms sat in the back of the classroom. Jaclyn refused to sit down or even go near a chair. I tried to gently lead her. I tried to persuade her. I tried to reason with her. She wouldn't budge.

By this time, all eyes in the room were focused on this little power struggle. I could almost hear the clucks of disapproval from the moms of the well-behaved children. I began to wrestle Jaclyn into a chair; finally, we compromised with her sitting on my lap. This left two-year-old Christy free, and she began ramming her stroller into the furniture. The teacher gamely tried to ignore her and continue teaching, until Christy got a running start with the stroller and headed directly for her. I leaped from my seat and grabbed the stroller when it was no more than an inch from the teacher's bottom. This was the opportunity Jaclyn was waiting for; she ran out of the classroom and into the hall, where she tried desperately to get outside, all the while screaming and crying. The teacher shut the classroom door firmly behind us.

All the cajoling and comforting in the world would not get Jaclyn to budge, so we headed home. I was frustrated once again by her behavior. I was so sure that I knew what was best for her that I wouldn't concede this battle. I dragged her to Chinese school every week, and, afraid of disappointing me, she went with only minimal protesting.

But slowly it began to dawn on me that her aversion to Chinese school fit with other of her behaviors. She refused to eat the same Chinese food that she loved at home when we took her to local Chinese restaurants. I was dismayed by the way she ran from the room, shielding her eyes, when we watched the video of our trip to China to adopt her. Now that she had words to express herself, I wanted to know more about her life in the orphanage. But all my gentle inquiries were met with hostile defiance on her part.

"GO AWAY, GUALING!" she would say in furious dismissal of my questions. She was intractable about this; she was not going to talk about her past. She turned her head if I showed her pictures from her formerly prized book of photos of her friends in China. Then the album that she had looked at several times a day while in China, repeating her friends' names over and over, could not be found.

But a few days later I realized that the photo book had not disappeared in its entirety. Jaclyn did not see me watching her as she sat huddled in a corner of her room staring intently at a few pictures in her hand. "Xiao Mei Mei," she said softly while gently stroking the photos. She had removed from the book the pictures containing him and secreted them away.

I shook my head in bewilderment over her tenaciousness in hanging on to this memory. I wondered how long it would be before she forgot him. After all, I reasoned, she's only four years old. She'll soon get caught up in her new life and totally forget about her past, even him. Which meant only one thing: I still didn't know Jaclyn at all.

Chapter Seven

Jaclyn's Baby

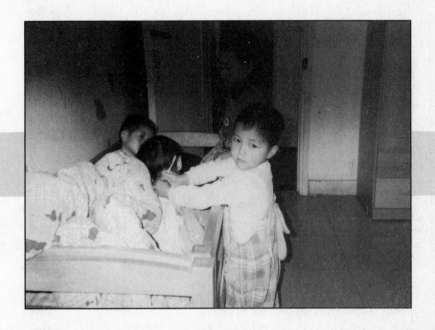

Being deeply loved by someone gives you strength, while loving someone
deeply gives you courage.
—Lao Tzu

On a warm September morning, my sister Laura called with thrilling news: their referral from China had finally arrived. She was to be the mother of a three-year-old girl named Tuan Ming, who was, as she had requested, from Jaclyn's orphanage. Laura tried to love the solemn-faced child with delicate features that stared back at her from the referral photo, but her heart was wary. The loss of the referral of Jin Xun Li had hurt her deeply. It is hard to explain how you can bond so deeply with a photo of an unknown child on the other side of the earth, how your arms can ache to hold them, how familiar and dear to you they become through the briefest scraps of information about who they are. And I shared her sorrow. After all, I had actually held Jin Xun Li in my arms. I had heard her giggle. I had heard her sobs. She had a big chunk of my heart, too.

Carl Hiller, an adoptive father and close friend, had listened to my pain and with determination and ingenuity sought to find the child we so needed to know about. He contacted every adoption agency, every Internet site, every adoptive parents' group he could think of, seeking information on Jin Xun Li. Had anyone received the referral of this child? Did anyone know her whereabouts? Weeks went by and there was no news. Finally, when he had nearly given up, a small adoption agency in Seattle contacted him. She had been placed with one of their families. They would not give us the family's name as it was confidential, but they would pass along our desperate pleas for contact with them. At least we knew she had a home. She had been placed with a single mother in New Jersey. But we still mourned for her and were puzzled by God's logic. How could this placement possibly be better for her than being part of the extended family of her old best friend? Much to our surprise, we still did not hear from her new mom. She apparently was not anxious to know us.

I was delighted when Laura invited me to come with them on their adoption journey to China. I knew she secretly longed for big sister reassurance from one who had been there. Usually pragmatic, I dismissed the cost of making such a trip and all the practical issues like lost time from work and coverage for mom on the home front. I had missed out on too many important moments in life because I had so many practical reasons not to do something; I was not going to miss out on this. It was the chance of a lifetime, the opportunity to witness the miracle of adoption from the sidelines. I wanted to include Jaclyn on this trip, too. I knew from other adoptive moms that children often bonded more readily with other children, and hoped that Jaclyn, whose native language was still intact, could help ease the first few days for Tuan Ming by helping with translation. We would only go for the first week, leaving the new family a week alone together to bond.

My parents gently suggested that this return might wreak havoc with Jaclyn's fragile emotional security. They worried that she would misconstrue the trip as one to return her to the orphanage. Still unsure of how much she comprehended my words, I asked her several times if she wanted to go back to China to bring Tuan Ming home. I also had our Chinese friend Fong explain to her that she was not going back to live but just for a one-week visit. Did she want to go? Her answer each time was a resounding yes, but she had her own reason for going: she wanted to see Xiao Mei Mei.

When she had first spoken of him in China, I was almost amused by her fixation on him. I had been sure he would soon be forgotten. After all, children are notoriously self-involved. I was sure that learning a new language, learning how to be part of a family again, adapting to a new school and a new home, would block out all the shadows from her past. But it was now evident that a shadow had come to live with us instead. A shadow named Xiao Mei Mei.

Not a day went by without her talking of him, reminiscing about him, worrying about him. He was more than just a part of her past; he was a part of her heart. And slowly he began to worm his way into mine.

At breakfast the next Saturday, Jaclyn began my instruction in Chinese. "Say *goonay*," she would say, attempting to teach me the Chinese word for "girl."

"*Goonay*," I would repeat back as she laughed uproariously at my slaughtering of the subtle nuances in the language. Kate, Christy, and Rick tried to get in on the game, too, much to her delight.

"Say *itsu*," she then said slowly.

"*Itsu*," I repeated back, sure I had slaughtered the word for "boy" that she was trying to teach.

Like any good teacher, she tried to illustrate her lesson, in this case by bringing out her photo album and pointing to her orphanage friends, indicating by using the Chinese word which were girls and which were boys. Gender was not evident from the photos, since many of the clothes seemed unisex and everyone had the same haircut. She then brought the conversation back, as always, to Xiao Mei Mei. Jaclyn, being the clear authority in this area, told the girls in a conspiratorial whisper that she was sure that Xiao Mei Mei was a boy because "he have little pee-pee in the front." She then illustrated by holding up her tiny pinkie finger and showing us just the top joint of it. She now had the girls' full attention. She then continued, "Just like . . . DADDY!" The stricken look on my macho Italian husband's face was priceless.

I busied myself packing for most of the day, so I would be ready when we got travel approval. I put the big suitcases we would take with us in the basement where they would be out of the way. After dinner, Jaclyn wandered down to watch as I folded her clothes and placed them in the suitcase. She disappeared upstairs and then came back with a stash of unopened McDonald's toys. Ever since her first Happy Meal she had refused to rip open the packages of little toys, as her sisters did, and instead left the wrapping intact and hid them away. It was only one of her hoarding behaviors. I found secret stashes of potato chips, her favorite food, hidden all over the house. I tried to ignore these actions, hoping that when she felt safe, her need for stockpiles would diminish. But I had misread her intentions; she wasn't saving them for herself. "This-a-ones for Xiao Mei Mei. He never get little toy," she said. And with that, wordlessly, she piled them into the suitcase.

"Jaclyn," I said gently, "are you excited about going back to China and seeing your old friends?" I knew this was wishful thinking on my part; she had not spoken a good word about the country since we had been home. But my own love for China made me determined to change her negative opinion of her homeland.

"I happy I see Jin Xun Li and Xiao Mei Mei," she said.

"Jaclyn, remember I told you that Jin Xun Li was adopted? She doesn't live there anymore. She lives in America with her new family now."

Jaclyn furrowed her brow in confusion. "Why Jin Xun Li get a mama when she can put clothes on and Xiao Mei Mei no get a mama and he can't do it and need help?"

I shook my head mutely; there was no right answer to her question.

"Xiao Mei Mei—he so cold all the time. Bad boys hit him. Kids take food from him like this," she said, furiously pantomiming the action. "He little. He go like this in the cold," and with that she pantomimed teeth chattering.

"Why was he cold, Jaclyn?" I said, puzzled, since Gualing was known for its temperate, springlike year-round climate.

"In Gualing, no jammies," she said. "They make you take this a-one off at night," she said, indicating her clothes. "They make you sleep just in this-a one," indicating her panties. "No little shirt even!"

"Were you cold there, too, Jaclyn?" I gently queried.

"Yes," she said, her eyes far away with memory. "I cold and hungry all the time." And then, taking a deep breath, she went on to explain further. "Window broken where Jaclyn sleep. This-a ones come in"—she fluttered her fingers like tiny flying bugs. "I have itch-yous all over. Rain come in and get kids bed wet. In the morning, teacher say kids peep the bed. But they not! It rain!" She shook her head in disgust. I knew from her earlier accounts of orphanage life that strict punishment was meted out to those who wet the bed.

"In Gualing no cereal. No milk. No chip," she said. "Only drink water. Some water 'tummy ache water' and make my tummy hurt. Milk just for babies. But one time I get apple for treat." She became more agitated, anxious for me to understand the difference between her life now and her past.

"In Gualing no dolls. No toys. No teddy bears," she said. "In China, *pon-nee* STANKY!" It was hard to refute that one; the open trench toilets were hard to forget.

"GO AWAY, GUALING," she said, waving both hands in furious dismissal. "China YUCKY!"

I could tell by the set look on her face that there was no convincing her otherwise, so I sent her upstairs to get ready for bed. About twenty minutes later, I followed. I could hear her talking but wondered whom she was talking to as both her sisters were downstairs watching TV. I peeked around the door and watched as she sat in the big white rocking chair gently rocking her teddy bear, wrapped in her favorite blanket.

"I sing for you, Xiao Mei Mei," she said, gently stroking the bear's head. Then, with her limited English she muddled through the first few verses until she got to the familiar refrain:

Yes, Jesus LUBBA YOU!
Yes, Jesus LUBBA YOU!

At the end of the song, she kissed her teddy bear so tenderly I could hardly stand to watch it. Seeing me there in the doorway, she put her teddy bear down and motioned for me to crawl into her bed with her. She fixed her gaze on my face and said without preamble, in a very matter-of-fact tone, "Jack-win have two mamas." I inhaled sharply but nodded my head yes, wondering where this was headed.

"One go-away mama. One this-a mama," she said, indicating me. I nodded yes. Then she added, "I no want go-away mama. I want this-a mama."

"Oh, Jaclyn, I'm so glad because I want you, too," I said, holding her close to me and smoothing her hair with my fingers.

"I scared," she said softly.

"What are you scared of?"

"I scared this-a mama go away," she whispered. I tried to reassure her, but I knew that my words meant nothing; only my permanence in her life would bring her the sureness of knowing that I would never leave her.

I prayed with the girls each night. Jaclyn would listen intently while I did so, but I did not know what, if anything, she understood about these spiritual renderings. On this night I got my answer.

When I finished my prayer, to my surprise Jaclyn began one of her own: "Dear God, Xiao Mei Mei sad. Xiao Mei Mei *cruela* [cries]. Xiao Mei Mei no daddy. Xiao Mei Mei no Katie. Xiao Mei Mei no Christy." Then she was silent.

It did not surprise me that her first prayer was for Xiao Mei Mei. I choked back tears, saying, "Oh, Jaclyn, I know it is sad that Xiao Mei Mei doesn't have a family or a mama."

She then looked me directly in the eyes and whispered, "Jack-win is Xiao Mei Mei's mama."

With every ounce of willpower I had, I held my face in a neutral expression so as to conceal my reaction to this startling declaration. She always searched my face carefully when she spoke of sensitive issues, so I was afraid to respond in a way that would make her not want to tell me any more. She was sensitive to the nuances of my moods and feelings; I knew that if she thought she had upset me she would shut down. She needed to be able to trust me with her past.

I held back my choking sobs until I got downstairs. Rick took one look at my stricken face and asked me what was wrong. But I shook my head mutely. If I opened the floodgates on all the sadness that I felt about where she had been and what she had been through, if I gave in to my grief about all the children still there like Xiao Mei Mei, my tears would never end.

That evening was a turning point for both of us. Jaclyn was now ready to tell me about her past, to trust me with the knowledge of who she really was. And I determined that I would find a home for the child that she called, from this night on, "her baby."

Chapter Eight

Jaclyn's First Birthday

I have spread my dreams under your feet,
tread softly because you tread on my dreams.
—W. B. Yeats

October 1, 1999, *was a momentous* day of celebration in the People's Republic of China; it was the fiftieth anniversary of the takeover by the Communists. It was also a momentous day of celebration in the Champnella household because it was Jaclyn's first birthday celebration. She had no idea what to expect, as she had never had a birthday celebration before.

She awoke in the morning and savored the treat of being able to wear a party dress to school. She came down the stairs beaming as she shyly showed off her light blue and white striped dress with a full, puffy slip underneath, her fancy white tights, and her favorite black patent leather party shoes.

As always, she was full of questions. "How old Jack-win?" she asked me. I had the same question. Her age had been a puzzle from the beginning. The orphanage had guessed at it, since she was not an infant when she arrived there. She was almost exactly the same size as Jin Xun Li, but we knew she had to be slightly older as she had at one time helped care for her. This was not a case of a child who was diminutive in stature; Jaclyn had a barrel chest and a solid, muscular build. We had taken her to both a pediatrician and a dentist to help us assess her age. We even had a bone scan done, which placed her birth date at May of 1995 with an error factor of six months.

Armed with this new information, we were torn about what to do. We wanted to keep her assigned birth date after the moving story the orphanage director told us about how she had chosen it. So we now had to decide whether to make her officially six months older or younger than her probable age. After consulting with the school social worker, we decided to make her younger in case she needed to be held back in school. I figured this way she would thank me when she turned thirty. I hedged often in telling her age, depending upon the reason for the question. Jaclyn had picked up on this, and wanted this mystery clarified.

I told her the age that we were celebrating, but she was not willing to let go of the issue so easily. "I hear you say five. Jack-win five or four?" she demanded. Finally she tired of my fruitless attempts to sort it out. "Why you not know?" she demanded in frustration. And I, feeling equally frustrated, told her the truth: "Your China mama didn't tell anyone how old you were." I knew as soon as I said it that I should not have spoken this truth out loud.

But a part of me resented the fact that even this basic piece of identity had been denied her. Was it too much to ask that her mother pin a note to her with her birth date, just her birth date, on it? But the few facts I knew about her abandonment made it seem likely that she had not been expected to survive. If you left your child in the woods, presumably to die, you wouldn't be thinking about providing the information necessary to start a new life.

"Call her on phone, Mama. Tell her. Tell her how old I!" Jaclyn demanded. I knew she meant for me to ask her mama this question.

"I can't, Jaclyn," I said. "I don't know her name." She was silent.

Then, anxious not to let this issue mar the day, she proclaimed herself age four with finality and moved on. She proudly helped me carry trays of cupcakes to the car for all her classmates. She solemnly promised her sisters that she would save one for each of them. After carefully surveying them all, she pointed out to me the one that she wanted her best friend, Olivia, to have.

When she came home she shrieked in delight at her first piece of real mail: a birthday card from Rick's mother. "Thank-a you, Grandma, for HAPPY BIRTHDAY!" she squealed in delight to her on the phone. There was a second card addressed to her, but it had an unfamiliar return address. When she opened it, pictures tumbled out. Pictures of Jin Xun Li and her new family. Jaclyn studied them intently. Jin Xun Li's mom had finally called me, after I repeatedly cajoled her adoption agency. I had promised that I would send the pictures and the video we'd taken of Jin Xun Li in China, a priceless treasure to adoptive parents who have missed so much of their child's past, if she would just call me. She was hesitant about making the contact, thinking it better for her child to put the past behind her. I had sent her the pictures and she had promised pictures in return, but I had not been hopeful that I would ever hear from her again, so this card was a welcome surprise. Jaclyn grasped this connection with her past with both hands, refusing to put the pictures down even for a minute. She even clutched the card and pictures throughout dinner, eating with one hand so she could do so.

She finally allowed me to look at the photos, too, and I could hardly believe what I saw. The beaming little girl in the daisy-covered hat was hardly recognizable as the same child we had seen so pitifully sobbing for a home and family just a few short months ago.

After dinner, Jaclyn disappeared upstairs with the pictures. Days later I discovered where they were hidden—inside the very bottom flap in Jaclyn's favorite Barney book, which had been hidden in her secret backpack of cherished treasures.

We had invited a few close friends and our family for a casual celebration dinner. Jaclyn was delighted to see her favorite uncle, Jeff, among the guests.

"Jaclyn, tell Uncle Jeff what you call our baby," I prompted. Jaclyn had recently picked up on our comments about Christy's delicate fingers and had nicknamed her "Baby Angel Fingers." Jaclyn looked at me in confusion as if the answer to this question was evident. "I call my baby Xiao Mei Mei," she said resolutely.

I clarified my request: "Tell Uncle Jeff what you call Christy."

"Christ-ta-tee *you* baby," she said firmly. "*My* baby still in China." There was no escaping this painful loss, even on this festive day of celebration.

My family knew that this was Jaclyn's first real birthday and came loaded down with gifts. Jaclyn dug into the pile with relish, ripping the paper with excitement and giggling with delight over each item. Like all kids, she saved the cards for last. After they were all opened, she entered into protracted negotiations with Kate over which gifts Kate wanted. Her sister easily bought into this deal, and Jaclyn was stunned when I interceded and told her that the gifts were all for her and she didn't have to share. But later I did notice that Kate had somehow wound up with a nice set of markers.

Jaclyn's favorite gift by far came in the form of a phone call. I overheard Rick answer the phone and could hardly believe it when I heard him say, "Hello, Jin Xun Li!" To which the child replied, "NO Jin Xun Li! Samantha!" When Jaclyn realized who was on the phone, her face broke into a huge smile. She raced to the phone, nearly knocking Rick off balance in the process, and grabbed the receiver in excitement. Although we coached Jaclyn to speak to her in Chinese, to our amazement the girls spoke to each other in English. Jin Xun Li was even more fluent than Jaclyn.

Jin Xun Li rattled on, in a manner typical of a four-year-old, about her new mom and her new house. Jaclyn, when she could get a word in edgewise, only spoke about one thing: her baby, Xiao Mei Mei. She questioned Jin Xun Li over and over about how he was after she left and about what had happened to him. She grew more frantic for answers as Jin Xun Li babbled on about other topics; Jaclyn continually tried to redirect the conversation.

After she hung up, she informed me, "Jin Xun Li got mama! Jin Xun Li got house! Jin Xun Li got toys! Jin Xun Li got sisters!" I told her that was wonderful and then gently asked what news she had relayed about Xiao Mei Mei.

"She tole me Xiao Mei Mei sad. Xiao Mei Mei *cruela* for Jaclyn. Xiao Mei Mei NO mama." She thought about this, her face downcast and etched in sadness, and then asked me hopefully, "Xiao Mei Mei get a mama when he get big?" I stood there mutely; once again I had no answers.

Later that night I watched Jaclyn blow out the candles on her first cake. And I had a fleeting wish for her to get all of them in one breath so that her wish would come true. Certainly, if anyone deserved to have her wish granted, she did. Alas, it was not to be. She was afraid to stand too close. She made lots of whiffs without blowing even one out. It was hard to let her keep trying, but I knew that moms couldn't always rush in and fix things, that important life lessons are learned through perseverance. And I knew that if I was patient, she would in her own time, with her own style, succeed. Finally, on the umpteenth try, she got the last one.

I thought about the analogy between her many tries and her life so far. This was a child whose wishes in life hadn't been granted easily or without effort. This was a child who had to keep trying, over and over, to make her dreams come true. And I knew that the sheer force of will that she had in spades, the same strong will that made me sometimes want to throttle her, would serve her in good stead in life. She would stand there and keep trying. She would not give up. She would not ask for help. She would persevere. I had no doubt that she had the power within her to make her wishes come true.

We all do. The journey to becoming her mother had shown me, beyond any doubt, the power that each of us has inside us. We have the ability to make things happen. We can shape our destinies. Even when others scoff at our attempts, we can still do difficult things and travel to unknown places and return both stronger and wiser. We can trust our own strength. We can trust God. We have to believe that within us is the greatest power on this earth: the power of a mother's love. It can move mountains, whatever form they may take in our lives.

I'd come to realize lately that the real regrets I had about my life so far were not about all the bad things that had happened but about all the good things I could have made happen and didn't.

It was just one of the many insights I'd had in finding my way to Jaclyn.

Before going to bed, Jaclyn came and gave me a fierce hug. "Thank-a you, Mama, for happy birthday. There no happy birthday in China. I wish my baby have happy birthday." Even on this day of joy, there was sadness that remained rooted in her soul. One thing still marred her happiness in her new life: her baby was still there. And that meant everything to her.

Chapter Nine

The Greatest Love

Tough people are not born; they are made when no one is there
to wipe their tears.
—Unknown

As our trip to China neared, Jaclyn's quest to bring Xiao Mei Mei home became more ceaseless and more desperate. Days before we were to leave, the girls sat at the kitchen table finishing their dinner while I started the dishes.

Jaclyn watched me and then said, "Xiao Mei Mei could wash-ee the dishes. He a good boy." She was always selling his virtues.

She waited for me to comment, and when I didn't, she added, "I hold him on my lap for dinner so he not need chair." She had noticed that we only had five chairs for our table and was anxious to vanquish any obstacle.

I still was silent, so she moved on to her next plan: "Christ-ta-tee could go live with Nana and Pops. Then Xiao Mei Mei come here. He sleep Christ-ta-tee bed." Christy continued eating, oblivious to the life-altering plans under consideration, but Kate howled in protest. "NO, Jaclyn, we are *not* giving Christy away!" she said angrily.

"Christ-ta-tee *you* baby, Kate. But Xiao Mei Mei *my* baby, and he still be in China," Jaclyn explained in an attempt to mollify her.

But Kate was angry now. "NO, Jaclyn! I love Christy!"

Surprised by the vehemence in Kate's reaction, Jaclyn modified her proposal again: "Christ-ta-tee go live with Jeff-er and Lola. They nice. She like it there."

"No, Jaclyn," I told her firmly. "Christy is part of this family, just as you are. She is staying here always, just like you."

But Jaclyn was not ready to give up yet. "Mama," she begged, "you be Xiao Mei Mei's mama? *Penache? Penache?*" I tried to evade her gaze and did not answer her. I knew that this was what she dreamed of, what she longed for, but I was not able to commit to another child. My life had spun in circles since her arrival. Our family rhythm was still too tenuous, too unsteady, to think of adding more to the imbalance. But hearing her desperate pleas pained me deeply. I felt as if I had no tears left; her frantic advocacy for this pathetic little boy was heartbreaking.

"Mama, he *my* baby," she said yet again, as if this was still not properly understood. Then, considering this further, she asked, "He ever live in my tummy?"

"No, Jaclyn, you're just a little girl. He grew in a China mama's tummy, just like you did."

"But he still *my* baby!" she added vehemently. And I, of all people, could not refute this. Didn't I, too, have babies of my own that did not grow inside me?

But Jaclyn was not done yet. The next morning at breakfast she presented a new plan: "Mama," she said, feigning brightness, "Jack-win go live with Jeff-er and Lola. Then Xiao Mei Mei come here and have this-a mama."

Her words stunned me. I knew the depth of this sacrifice because I knew more than anyone about her fierce love and steadfast devotion to "this-a mama." She could not hide from me her fear, always below the surface, that "this-a mama" go away. That she was willing to give up her own family and home was unfathomable. Greater love hath no child.

Her determination strengthened my resolve to use this trip as a means of getting more information about Xiao Mei Mei and to try to get him registered for adoption. I knew how difficult this would be, given how few children were afforded this opportunity. And from what I had seen, I believed that those that were more desirable—the cutest, the brightest, the most alert—were a small percentage. I knew that even getting him registered would be a long shot.

On an overcast day in October, we left our home in Michigan for Beijing, China. Jaclyn and I arrived at the airport first and waited impatiently for the arrival of the parents-to-be, Laura and Jeff. I saw both excitement and apprehension in Laura as we took our seats for the thirteen-hour flight ahead.

Jeff, always high energy, always looking for ways to be helpful, relieved me of Jaclyn as soon as the seat belt sign went off and began walking the aisles of the plane with her. Jeff's warm smile and friendly demeanor ensured that he did not go anywhere alone; he knew many of the passengers well by the time the plane landed. Laura closed her eyes and tried to rest. The past few days of harried packing and arranging for Kirsten and Elise's care while she was gone had left her spent.

Sleep eluded me. I watched the clouds outside the window and tried to focus on the promise I had resolutely made to myself: I would not leave China without getting Xiao Mei Mei registered for the adoption program. I knew I could not do it alone. But it was up to me; I had no one to turn to for help. Laura and Jeff needed to concentrate their energies on their new child, Tuan Ming.

I closed my eyes and prayed, and the feeling of aloneness disappeared. I prayed first for Xiao Mei Mei. He was, without a doubt, the most pathetic child I had ever seen. When I saw in my mind's eye pictures of children in refugee camps I thought about the most haunting faces and knew that those faces were his. His ears seemed huge next to his tiny shrunken skull. His eyes seemed old and lifeless for one so young. He was a walking skeleton. He was so tiny that he shared a chair at the orphanage preschool. Unlike Jaclyn, who was seated front row center, he sat in his half of the chair in the back of the room, not troubling anyone for attention, I suspect. His way of crying without making any sound, of letting tears just stream down his face, was heartwrenching. I believed that part of the reason Jaclyn loved him so was that she could sense how vulnerable he was. She hugged him so fiercely as if to instill in him, through her touch, some of her strength and will and hopefulness.

I remembered how he had followed her everywhere and how she never let go of his hand. I thought of how they fell asleep clutching hands. And although she had talked of him constantly in China, I'd had no real idea of the depth of her love until I watched her say good-bye to him. I prayed that he had survived the heartbreak of losing his fierce protector. I prayed for God to send guardian angels to keep him safe. I prayed that he had somehow remained hopeful about finding his own family.

I also prayed for a special mother's heart, one that could see beyond his sad little exterior into the soul and heart of this extraordinary little boy. I prayed for a mother who knew that her love had the power to heal a broken spirit. A mother who could look into a face that the world might call homely and see only a beautiful child looking back. A mother who had the courage to do something difficult and the faith to see it through. A mother who could hold back a piece of her heart and rejoice for him if he ended up, after all her efforts, with another family. A mother who knew that the real goal here, the one that transcended her own, was to find him a home. A mother who could love him the way Jaclyn did.

I prayed for those whose help I needed to get him adopted, the professionals in this field who knew too well the heartache of motherless children. The ones who could so easily become burned out and jaded. The ones who knew how to work the system and whose only reward was to watch from the sidelines as families were made. The miracle workers. Their names were Snow and Andrea from the Great Wall staff. I prayed that they would be touched once again by a plea for one special child.

I prayed for the officials at the China Center for Adoption Affairs. I could only imagine the mountain of paperwork they faced daily. Four persons to process more than six thousand adoptions a year without the benefit of computers or advanced technology? It was overwhelming even to envision. I could only imagine their frustration when they were asked to abandon those important tasks and make exceptions for still another child. I knew how easy it must be to say no. But I prayed that once again they would have hearts filled with mercy so they could look away from the rules for a moment to let another child slip through. I prayed that they would not be the insurmountable obstacle in all of this.

And then I admit that I prayed for myself. I had been raised never to ask others for help or favors. I prayed that God would make me fearless in asking for help this time. I prayed that I would be strong enough to advocate determinedly for this child. I prayed for the strength that comes from a mother's love so I would be tenacious and resolute. I prayed that I would not get discouraged, that I would not accept that there was no way. I determined to use my strong voice to give a voice to this child, who was so silent.

But I prayed most fervently for Jaclyn. She had tirelessly, ceaselessly reminded us of Xiao Mei Mei. She would not forsake him. I thought of the stockpile of all her McDonald's toys, still in their wrappers, that she had brought to give to him. I thought about her desperation when she realized that she had exhausted all avenues she could think of and then was willing to give him her own place in our family. Although I had done everything I could think of to prepare her, I couldn't imagine how she would be able to say good-bye to him again. Her mind understood that he was not coming with us. But her heart could not. She loved him beyond reason; she loved him like a mother.

Chapter Ten

China, Round 3

Who travels for love finds a thousand miles not longer than one.
—Japanese proverb

After a night of fitful sleep, our bodies unused to the time shift, we gathered to meet the rest of the travel group for breakfast. The group was excited about their glimpses of China and couldn't wait to see more. Jaclyn stared at those who extolled the beauty of China as if they had lost their minds.

One of the first-time moms proudly showed off a picture of her soon-to-be daughter. Jaclyn peered at it, anxious to see what had made the adults "ooh" and "ahh." The woman stooped down and held the photo out to Jaclyn saying, "Do you want to see my baby?"

Jaclyn studied the photo intently while the mother beamed. Jaclyn then opened her backpack, pulled out a photo, and approached the woman again. "I have a baby, too," said Jaclyn. "Do you want to see *my* baby?" The woman admired Xiao Mei Mei, and Jaclyn beamed. But she was clearly anxious about everything and was asking me constantly what would happen next. And over and over, the question came, "When will I see Xiao Mei Mei?"

Having gotten nowhere with me, she was now relentless in lobbying Laura and Jeff to adopt Xiao Mei Mei. "Tuan Ming stay in China. Get Xiao Mei Mei," she implored. "He a good boy!"

"No, I can't leave Tuan Ming here," Laura replied patiently for what seemed to be the hundredth time since breakfast. "She is my daughter. I have to bring her home."

"OK," Jaclyn conceded. "You can get *two*. You get Tuan Ming, and Jeff-er can get Xiao Mei Mei." If only it were as simple as that. She was frustrated by our refusal to give in; we were equally tired of her ceaseless lobbying.

Our new guide, Sonia, appeared while we were finishing breakfast. The families swarmed her, demanding to know when they would get their babies.

"Tomorrow morning we will go to the Office of Civil Affairs and the babies will be given to you there," Sonia said. "But I have made special arrangements for you to see them for just a few moments today. The orphanage is permitting us to stop there and see the children on our way to the hotel." The parents murmured in surprise. Some of the moms began to fix their makeup and smooth out their travel clothes. I flashed back to the day we first met Jaclyn. We had been told as soon as the plane landed that we were to get her that same day. We, too, had been taken by surprise. We had been driven first to the hotel, where Rick and I had raced around frantically trying to make ourselves presentable. After all, first impressions count. Remembering, I didn't say anything to those who were so concerned about a baby's first impression of them.

We arrived at the orphanage and were quickly spirited upstairs to where the children waited; there was no time to look around. There were several single parents, and as an extra, I wanted to make sure that they all had pictures of this first moment. We stood in an open hallway as each child was brought out. The workers spoke the names in Chinese, and the corresponding parent would rush forward, arms open, and claim their child.

Then a tiny girl was brought down the dingy hallway. She was dressed in a heavy brown corduroy dress and looked as if she was in shock. She did not cry; her face was frozen in terror. It was Tuan Ming. Laura exclaimed over her beauty and knelt down in front of her and held out a snack for her. Tuan Ming moved into the protective arc of Laura's arms and took the snack from her. Laura picked her up and held her gently. Tuan Ming cowered in terror when Jeff came to her, so he wisely contented himself with being an onlooker.

Given her persistent nature, I had thought Jaclyn would run to find Xiao Mei Mei as soon as we entered the orphanage courtyard. But Jaclyn was terrified now that she was back in the place that still held so many bad memories for her. She clung to me in an uncharacteristic manner, her bravado and natural exuberance gone. She lifted her arms up for me to hold her and hid her face in my shoulder.

Staff recognized her and greeted her warmly.

"NO!" she would say fiercely in response to their attempt to touch her, to talk to her, to see her. I couldn't carry her for very long, and when

I set her down, she buried her face in my legs and would not even grant them a glance. Her eyes were filled with anger. She was not ready to make nice.

I was embarrassed by her reaction. I was always conscious of showing my best manners when I was a visitor in this country, and I tried to coax her to do likewise, but she was having none of it. She had shared very little with me about her life in the orphanage, and the staff all seemed kind and genuinely loving. I did not yet understand how deep her scars were, how much she had endured here.

I asked her to tell the staff member escorting us that we wanted to see Xiao Mei Mei, but she refused. She would not speak Chinese, she would not speak to any of them, and she would not speak to me. Her face was frozen, her mouth set. I was frustrated by her refusal to help in this reunion that I knew she desperately wanted. I tried to ask them myself, saying "Xiao Mei Mei" over and over as they stared at me blankly.

I commandeered Sonia, even though she was busy trying to interpret for all the families, to help me. She asked in Chinese, but her requests were met by blank stares, too. Then I spotted Jaclyn's former teacher. "Xiao Mei Mei?" I said, and she immediately walked with Jaclyn and me to the hallway where Jaclyn had lived. Laura, with Tuan Ming perched on her hip, and Jeff hurried over, too. They were anxious to meet this child we had all heard so much about.

He was sitting in exactly the same spot he had been when we last saw him. On a hard wooden bench in the dank TV room, he stared blankly at the snowy picture on the TV screen, as did the twenty or so other children seated there. A local woman had donated hand-knit sweaters, and he was the recipient of one; it was bright pink, which matched nicely with the pink shoes he was wearing on the wrong feet.

He looked at us solemnly and did not smile when he saw Jaclyn. She studied him shyly, still unable to speak. Jaclyn's face was set grimly, and she was agitated to see that his shoes were on the wrong feet. I assumed, given her solicitous, gentle smoothing of his clothes on our last visit, that she would remedy this for him. But Jaclyn is a cunning child. She held back this time and indicated that she wanted me to fix his clothes.

She wanted me to hold him and hug him. She wanted me to feel for myself the gentleness of his tiny body. She wanted me to love him.

I knelt down and changed his shoes as Jaclyn gently handed him a snack we had brought. He did not eat it right away, holding it firmly in his hand while looking steadily into her eyes. This upset her, too. She urged him to eat it, and when he did not she became more and more insistent in her prodding.

"The big boys take it if he not eat it now," she explained to me. We only had a moment so I quickly picked him up. I knew right away that Jaclyn was right about this child. There was something special about him. He nestled into my body, relaxing into my arms. He was so tiny and gentle. His big eyes locked on my own with such trust.

"He is so much cuter than his pictures," Laura said. She put down Tuan Ming for a moment as she relished the chance to hold him, too. Xiao Mei Mei also went to Jeff with the same trusting gaze and, desperate for love, snuggled into each of us. Jaclyn watched intently, her eyes still clouded in pain.

We were hurried along. This was an unscheduled visit, and it disrupted the careful synchrony of the day's events, so Jaclyn's former teacher insisted that we leave. Jaclyn was not ready to go. Xiao Mei Mei had not yet eaten his snack, and she was distressed by this. "It will be OK, Jaclyn," I said. "We gave treats for all the other kids, too." Jaclyn gave me a pitying glance, as if I was too naive to understand the system of which she was a veteran, a system in which older kids prey on those that are younger.

I promised her that we would return later in the week, and so she caressed his tiny cheek and then obediently took my hand and walked away. We had turned the corner and walked halfway down a long hallway when Jaclyn suddenly broke away from my grasp and ran back to where Xiao Mei Mei had been. I called for her to stop, but this made her run even faster, so I took off after her. She turned the corner and froze, the pain of what she saw literally stopping her dead in her tracks. Xiao Mei Mei was once again standing forlornly alone, silent tears cascading down his cheeks. Jaclyn turned her head, unable even to look. I began to cry, too, as did Laura, who had hurried to catch up with me.

As we were escorted out, I started my campaign immediately, begging any staff member who would listen for identifying information about Xiao Mei Mei so he could be registered for adoption. But there was no time for this now. I vowed to myself that on the return visit to the orphanage I would not leave without this information.

I know the staff must have felt bad that Jaclyn would not even look at them; it was more than a little embarrassing.

Back at the hotel, the group was excited, nervous, happy, and anxious, feeling all the emotions that you go through in becoming a family. But I couldn't read Jaclyn; it was as if her heart was frozen in grief.

I figured that at bedtime she might disclose more, and indeed she did. "I sad in my heart from see Xiao Mei Mei," she said. "He sad. He *cruela*. I knew he be sad! I knew he *cruela*!" I listened silently. There was no refuting this; we had both seen it with our own eyes.

"You see floor, Mama?" Jaclyn continued. "It all wet. They clean the floor. Xiao Mei Mei always fall when they clean the floor. He always fall on the wet. Who help him now [when] he fall? Jack-win not there help him. I tole you *nobody* help him!" I had not heard this before; now I added slipping on wet floors to the ever-growing list of concerns about this child.

"Soon as we go, big kids take his food. They always take his food." I nodded mutely. And then she added wistfully, "If Xiao Mei Mei have a mama, he have food every day." I had heard it all many times before, but it struck a nerve in my heart again. I promised her that I would try to find him a mama. I didn't know what else to do. But when her eyes met mine, I turned away. I knew that look. I knew it meant I wasn't doing enough. I knew it meant I had fallen short of what she expected. She wanted to take him now. She wanted him home with her. She wanted me to be his mother. But that was more than I could promise.

Laura and Jeff came to get us early in the morning for breakfast. This was adoption day; in just a few hours, Tuan Ming would be their daughter.

"I couldn't sleep," Laura said as we sat down at the table. "I woke up crying at three A.M., thinking of the kids at the orphanage. It was such a strange déjà vu feeling, since I recognized so many of them from the pictures and video you had of your last trip. I almost felt like I knew some of them."

"I couldn't sleep either," Jeff confessed. "You know what struck me about some of the kids? They had this look in their eyes, this flat, lifeless look. It was as if they had no expectations. As if there was a party going on that they had not been invited to. As if they knew they never would be. So many of them looked like that. I guess it comes from seeing so many parents come and go over the years and knowing that you are left behind. But that lifeless look, an expression that conveys the expectation of nothing, is hard to forget when it is on a child's face. A child's face should be filled with hope and expectations. I finally got out of bed and wrote a letter to our new daughter. I'm going to put it away for her until she gets older. As happy as we are, I know this will be a difficult day for her."

"But I thought your baby was darling, Jaclyn," Laura said. "He's so sweet. I loved holding him." Jaclyn smiled proudly.

"Can he talk?" I asked Jaclyn, as we had never heard him speak.

"He just little so he not talk too much. But he talk to Jack-win a little when I live in China," she said.

"I could not believe it when they took us to that hall and he was sitting in exactly the same place in that dreary TV room," I said. "I remember how Jaclyn recoiled from TV, as if watching it was a punishment, when we first adopted her. But seeing that old broken TV in that claustrophobic room helped me understand why. I thought it was odd when she said all they ever watched on it was soccer matches. Then I realized that our TV set in the hotel room has two channels that seem to show soccer continuously."

"Maybe after two years in the TV room, scientists will want to study him for ill effects," Jeff said, laughing in a gallows humor kind of way. "Or maybe he'll just make a great soccer coach."

We tried to make light of the situation, but the truth was that Jaclyn's anecdotes about him and her pleas for him had somehow infused all of us with love for Xiao Mei Mei. I couldn't believe how much I cared for him, how dear he had become to me. I could still feel the tiny warmth of him in my arms.

After breakfast, we headed over to the Office of Civil Affairs for the formal presentation of the children and to do the paperwork to legalize the adoptions. I was flooded with emotion as I entered that room to see the waiting children. The two older kids, Tuan Ming and a six-year old boy named Xi Lan, did not have caregivers to hold them. Xi Lan raced right over to his new dad and did not wait for the formal pass-off. After this clear breach of protocol, Jaclyn, who had known him well in the orphanage, reminded me again that he was a "silly boy." If only she had kept this verdict to herself. Instead, she marched over to the adoptive father and told him this, too. I think she expected him to give the child back, and she seemed mystified when he listened politely to her warning but still held tightly on to his new son.

Tuan Ming sat between caregivers on a worn rattan sofa; it was as if she was in shock. Tears trickled down her cheeks. Filled with fear, she stared at us silently. Laura was desperate to comfort her, but it really wasn't permissible until the workers gave the children to the parents. The babies all went easily to their new parents, and then the staff pushed Tuan Ming over to Laura, since she was reluctant to go. She let Laura hold her and tried hard not to cry. At one point the orphanage workers spirited her away from Laura and took her out into the hall for what appeared to be a pep talk, kind of like the Chinese version of "Hey, suck it up, kid." When she returned to the room, she went to Laura with her arms raised to be picked up. But if Jeff tried to get near her, she would push his hands away and cling to Laura. All in all, it seemed like a much better start than we'd had with Jaclyn.

Laura and Jeff had decided to name the child Willow after our older sister. I was pretty sure that this would give us a lock on being the only family in America with two members named Willow. We all began to call her this almost immediately, but Jaclyn, perhaps remembering her pain over her own name change, continued to call her Tuan Ming.

We walked over to the next required office and noticed that the orphanage workers were hiding along the route and watching us. Jaclyn was rude to all of them and gave them glares that made my blood run cold.

"Why they look?" she asked Jeff.

"Because they love Willow and they want to make sure she is OK," Jeff answered.

"They bad!" Jaclyn told Jeff vehemently. "They not love Tuan Ming. They not love Jack-win!" The workers approached us and tried to get Jaclyn to interpret for them, but she stubbornly refused to even look at them. She buried herself in my body but did reach out her hand to quickly snatch the apple one of the workers offered her.

We walked back to the hotel and up to the room. Willow was crying now, softly and steadily. Jaclyn watched it all and then motioned for Jeff to come into the hall with her.

"Tuan Ming sad. She not like Lola. She want a China mom," Jaclyn pronounced solemnly. Her projection of her own feelings onto this child gave me new insight into what she herself had gone through. "You need get her little potty. She too little go on big potty," Jaclyn advised him. So Jeff, Jaclyn, and I headed off to the local store to search for one, while Laura attempted to comfort the bereft child.

Jaclyn was anxious about our return visit to the orphanage and asked me constantly about when she would see her baby again. She asked over and over if he could have "this-a mama," meaning, of course, me. He continued to be all she talked about, although she was very kind and solicitous toward Willow. Jaclyn took her hand on the first day, and Willow seemed to take comfort in the familiarity of another child, and each day Jaclyn was anxious to see how Willow was progressing. Each morning as soon as she awoke, she raced down the hotel hallway to check on Willow.

"Tuan Ming like her mama now," Jaclyn reported one morning. "She just no like her daddy." This had been the same sequence of attachment we had experienced, and Jeff was patient, although his heart was saddened by the rejection, as Rick's had been.

As delighted as I was by the steady progress that Tuan Ming was making, her adoption was overshadowed in my mind by the task that still lay ahead. As anxious as Jaclyn was to return to the orphanage, I was more so. Each day I reiterated to Sonia that I must be permitted to return there before Jaclyn and I had to leave. I was not leaving China without starting the wheels in motion for Xiao Mei Mei's adoption registration.

Chapter Eleven

Introducing . . . Tan Dong Jin

The way to love anything is to realize that it might be lost.
—G. K. Chesterton

Our return visit to the orphanage was scheduled for Thursday after-noon. Jaclyn was thrilled, as was I, when I opened the suitcases with our donations for the orphanage; we filled four huge shopping bags. Jaclyn wanted to give all our gifts to Xiao Mei Mei. Instead, I let her pick out a special toy for him. She chose a tiny stuffed bear wearing a red coat and a blue hat. She removed from her own backpack several pictures of the two of them together that she wanted to leave with him, but as much as I prodded, she did not want to give him any of her with her new family. Having seen others adopted, I think she was sensitive to the envy factor and did not want to cause him any pain.

Jaclyn was apprehensive and anxious all day about when we were going to see Xiao Mei Mei. She begged me not to leave the toys and the clothes with the director and seemed to believe that he would not get them if we did. After standing there helplessly on my last trip to China, watching twenty children split a single candy, I was not going to be left without snacks to share this time. We had loaded up on candy and treats for the children.

Nevertheless, when we arrived at the orphanage, our bags of gifts were spirited away, much to Jaclyn's consternation. Later, a former vol-unteer at her orphanage that I befriended told me that Jaclyn had been right about this, too. Somehow the donations from parents rarely made their way directly back to the children. I speculated that maybe they were bartered on the black market for food and other necessities. Through careful maneuvering, however, I managed not to surrender the bag with the candy. Jaclyn had her heart set on giving treats to Xiao Mei Mei and her other friends. This, too, did not happen. The staff stopped us as we attempted to hand out the treats and said the children could not have them as it was nearly dinnertime. The bag was confiscated. Jaclyn was crushed.

When we entered the orphanage courtyard, Jaclyn immediately said,

"Oh look, Mama, that the boy who hit me. And that the lady [indicating one of the staff] that hit me all the time!" My face conveyed my shock as her words hit me like a blow. I looked into the eyes of a woman who had beaten my child and swallowed hard to fight the rage in the pit of my stomach so it would not eat me alive. Jaclyn saw my reaction and immediately stopped talking. Once again she refused to speak to any of the staff and even shouted a menacing "NO!" at the kindly director. I was mortified.

This time we headed directly to the TV room and, as we had expected, found Xiao Mei Mei sitting on a hard bench watching TV. He had on the exact same outfit that he had been wearing four days ago, but now the bright pink sweater was soiled and he looked grubby. When the kids spotted us, most of them rushed forward, and he was one of three left behind in the melee. Jeff went back to get him out of the room, while workers insisted that the other children remain in the doorway. Once again we had only a limited amount of time and I needed to use this time well. I needed to implore the director to get him registered for the adoption program.

"Jaclyn, we only have a few minutes," I told her. "You need to say good-bye to Xiao Mei Mei." Jaclyn stooped so that she was at eye level with the child and gently kissed and hugged him. He fixed his eyes on her and stared mutely. Jaclyn unbuttoned his sweater, slipped inside it the photographs that she had clutched in her hand, and buttoned it closed.

"The kids not take from him if in there," she said, pleased at her strategy. Her motions were slow and lifeless as if she were frozen in a state of emotional overload.

Jaclyn then placed the little teddy bear that we brought in his arms. "Now he not be so scared at night," Jaclyn said, as if to reassure herself. "He hold bear cause he not hold Jack-win's hand."

Laura, Jeff, and I could not resist savoring hugs from him once again. As I held him, I thought of him fleetingly as my son. I found out later that Laura had exactly the same thought. Reluctantly, we said good-bye. The other children waved and called good-bye after us. But Xiao Mei Mei stood there, silently staring, morose and forlorn. A staff member lifted his hand to help him wave, but he did so woodenly. Jaclyn turned on her heel, refusing to look back. I turned back several times to look at him, but his expression was unchanged.

But even Jaclyn with all her fortitude could not bear it. Once again she suddenly ran back and I again chased her. She rounded the corner and watched powerless, with a look of pain on her face, as a slightly older child snatched the bear from his hands. She turned on her heel and ran back to me as if she was unable to look again. Although I tried to comfort her by assuring her that the teacher who was there—and saw what had happened—would give the bear back to him, ultimately I had no words to reassure her; she had seen what she feared most with her own eyes.

I marched resolutely to the director's office. I had apologized in advance to the others in the group for my need to monopolize some of her valuable time to further my quest for information about Jaclyn's baby. The other parents were very understanding and put aside their interest in talking more to her about their children to aid me in my endeavor. I had to know his official name, his birth date, and if he was physically healthy enough to be eligible for adoption. I also had to convince them to use one of their few annual registrations in the adoption program for this child.

Over and over I repeated "Xiao Mei Mei" to the guide, Sonia, to the director, and to the assistant director. They continued to reply, much to my frustration, that there was no child there with that name. Finally I went out into the hallways to find the teacher and asked her to tell them which child I was asking about. She smiled over my confusion. She had recognized the name Xiao Mei Mei because she knew that this was Jaclyn's nickname for the child. His official name was Tan Dong Jin.

"Jaclyn," I said, still uncertain about the explanation, "did you know Xiao Mei Mei's name is really Tan Dong Jin?"

"Yes," she said, with a look that indicated I was truly simpleminded. I could have throttled her. Why in the world had she not told me his real name before?

"Lou Jiao is calling him Xiao Mei Mei," the teacher explained. "In Chinese it means 'very little, little sister.'" She chuckled over Jaclyn's confusion in calling a boy a little sister. "In some orphanages, all the children are given the last name of the director of the orphanage. Our system here is to give the child the last name of the part of the city that they are found in. Gualing is divided into five sections. So, Tan Dong Jin was found in the Tan part of town, Tuan Ming in the Tuan section. Lou Jiao is, of course, an exception to that as she came here knowing her birth name."

"*What?*" I exclaimed in shock.

"Yes, did you not notice how different her name is from the rest? When the policeman brought her here, she had already told him her name," the teacher continued. I felt weak-kneed as waves of regret washed over me. I had wrongly assumed that the policeman had assigned her name. How could I have been so cavalier about changing it? I later asked Jaclyn about this, and she confirmed that this was exactly what had happened. She gave me an incredulous look in response to my surprised face. Her look clearly said, "If you wanted to know, why in the world did you not ask me before?"

"Tan Dong Jin's birth date is 1-17-97, and he was brought to the orphanage on 12-17-98," the director told me, speaking through Sonia. "He can hear and speak. He is considered healthy. But I don't understand why you are so insistent that we register him for adoption. We registered him several months ago." I was shocked. Adoptive families rarely request boys. Given his pitiful appearance, I was sure that an institution this size would have saved their placements in the adoption program for a more appealing child. Waves of relief flooded me. My next step would be to meet with Julie Kerr, Great Wall's China coordinator, when we arrived in Beijing the next day and discuss how we could work together to find a family for him.

"I will try to find him a family when I get home to America," I told the director.

She was crestfallen at my words. "His papers have been at the China Center for Adoption Affairs for a few months now," she said. "I hope he doesn't have to wait much longer. It is my fervent wish that a family whose dossier is already at the CCAA will adopt him."

"Could we sponsor Tan Dong Jin?" I asked. "Could we provide monthly funds so that he was afforded special care?"

"That is not permitted here," the director replied firmly. "We feel it is best for the children to share and share alike."

Now I was crestfallen. How would we ever be able to find out what happened to him? Families from all over the world adopted from China. What if he was referred to a family in Australia, in the Netherlands, or in some other remote corner of the earth? My heart sank at the possibilities; I could not let him go. I hurriedly wrote a note with our name and address on it and put it together with a picture of him and Jaclyn. I secretly pressed the note into the teacher's hand.

"Please," I begged, "if he is adopted, please give this note to his new family and ask them to contact us. Jaclyn loves him so." Sonia translated my words, but the teacher did not acknowledge them. To do this was against the rules. The staff was not to intercede in any way in the adoption process; it was strictly forbidden. She turned away, the note still in her hand. With a heavy heart, I realized that I might never know the whereabouts of this child. I tried to tell myself that I was only doing this for Jaclyn, but I knew it was no longer true. I loved him, too. As much as I tried to deny it, as much as I was afraid to admit it, he had wormed his way into my heart. I could not bear the thought of never seeing him again.

The director then invited all the families to gather around a conference table. She gave a warm welcome to each family and child and addressed the group's questions. Jaclyn chose to exhibit her disrespect by crinkling a potato chip bag, noisily munching chips, and slurping water during the moving speech that followed. In spite of all my efforts to quiet her, she would not behave.

All during the week, Jaclyn puzzled over the fact that the six-year-old boy named Xi Lan was being adopted. She tried to sort out how the whole adoption process worked. "Mama," she asked, "how the lucky kids get adopted? How they get picked to get mamas?"

"I don't know," I answered honestly.

"Xiao Mei Mei not get a mama because he too little," she said firmly. "You have to be big like Jack-win and Xi Lan to get a mama." I didn't point out to her that most of the children being adopted were infants; she was desperate to find her own explanations for these puzzling events.

Although she had never questioned how she herself was chosen, she was surprised when she saw that a few of her former friends had been adopted and was quick to tell me her list of things that these little ones did wrong. The roster of misbehaviors primarily included hurting "her baby," crying at night out of fear of the dark, or wetting the bed.

"Why they want a naughty baby?" she asked. "Why they take that one and not take Xiao Mei Mei? He no trouble. He a *good* boy."

But this logic was very embarrassing as she took it upon herself to continually give Xi Lan's new dad the "heads up" on his little boy. I cringed over how many times she told his father that he was "yucky" and a "silly boy" and that she did not like him. Xi Lan's dad was experienced with children, so he listened to her seriously but considered the source of the information. She was often headstrong and difficult, while Xi Lan was a delight. Luckily, Xi Lan had no idea what she was saying, since he did not yet understand English, and he delighted in playing hide-and-seek with her under the dinner table and willingly shared toys with her on the long bus rides.

When we were ready to leave for Beijing, he proudly came to our room and presented her with a going-away gift. Jaclyn was quite moved and excited by this gesture. I used this opportunity to tell her, "See, he's not a yucky boy. He's a nice boy." She looked skeptical, but insisted immediately that we find something to give him. We headed out to the market, where she carefully surveyed all the goods and finally settled on a small hand-carved elephant. She proudly carried it all the way back to the hotel and ran to his room to give it to him.

When she came back, she was in a huff. I asked her what was wrong, and, arms folded across her chest, she said, "He no *xie xie* [thank you] Jack-win. He no thank-a-you Jack-win." Then, giving me her best I-told-you-so look, she said, as if to finally put the matter to rest, "He is a YUCKY boy!"

It reminded me of a saying my mother has: "A man convinced against his will is of the same opinion still." But who would have thought that Miss Jaclyn would become Miss Manners?

————

It was late at night when we landed in Beijing. At my request, Julie Kerr, the Great Wall coordinator, was waiting at the hotel to meet with me. I had to talk to her about Jaclyn's baby. We sat together in the hotel lobby, while Jaclyn shied away from Julie's gentle inquiries about her welfare.

"Cindy, I know you are interested in this boy Tan Dong Jin," Julie told me, "but I must advise you about the near impossibility of you or anyone in your family adopting him. Identified adoptions—those in which a particular child is requested, like Jaclyn's adoption—involve many special permissions and favors. The CCAA has placed new restrictions upon them. They dramatically slow the adoption process. You must remember that the files are all paper; there are no computers. To find one child's file out of thousands and one family's files out of hundreds of voluminous stacks is very difficult. For this reason, they are rarely permitted." Julie's tone was kind, but her words were firm.

"You must understand all the factors that are considered in the adoption process," she continued. "The CCAA has enacted new restrictions that will limit a family's ability to do multiple adoptions in a short time period. The officials strongly prefer that families wait one year between adoptions. Your sister has just adopted. You have only had Lou Jiao for a few months. They would not look favorably upon this. Another rule is that the first child adopted must be a U.S. citizen before the second dossier is filed." I knew that in Michigan the citizenship process often took a minimum of six months. This virtually guaranteed that neither Laura and Jeff nor Rick and I could adopt Tan Don Jin. We had all agreed that we wanted him to have a home as soon as possible.

"Julie, can you watch his file? Can you give me information about the family who adopts him so that I can share it with Jaclyn, so that she will know he is safe?" I implored.

"You know how difficult that is," she said with a tired smile. "The officials will not permit me access to files that do not belong to our agency's families. There is no way I can do that." I was downcast. I didn't know what else to do for him. I glanced over at Jaclyn and saw that she had fallen asleep on a nearby couch.

"I will say this," Julie said. "Very few families request a boy, especially one close to age three. There is a possibility that he will be waiting for a match for a long time." I was defeated.

"Thank you, Julie, for all you have done on behalf of our family and so many other families," I said while hugging her good-bye. "Tuan Ming is a precious little girl, and you did a marvelous job in helping to select her." Julie beamed at my praise.

"Good night, dear friend," I said as we parted. Julie's face was drawn and tired, but she was genuinely joyful at seeing Jaclyn again and in hearing about Tuan Ming's new life.

I watched her walk away with a sense of finality. It was not to be; there was no possibility Xiao Mei Mei would come to my family. I roused Jaclyn and headed up to our room.

I couldn't sleep, even though I knew our driver would be there to pick us up at 6:30 A.M. I waited to feel relief over the fact that I no longer had to struggle with whether Rick and I should adopt him. But all I felt was the sinking guilt at having failed Jaclyn. And failed him. We should have filed a dossier already to adopt Xiao Mei Mei.

And now he was gone.

As I tried to hurry an immobile Jaclyn in the morning, she looked at me and softly said, "I want to stay in China, Mama." My heart sank. Was our bond so tenuous that she did not really feel like my daughter? To me the connection felt so strong and sure.

"Jaclyn, you don't want to go home with me? Do you still wish for a Chinese mama?" I asked her gently.

"No," Jaclyn said impatiently, annoyed at my misunderstanding of her. "I want stay in China with this-a mama. I no want a China mama." Was this the same child who pronounced China "yucky" a week ago? The child who had utterly refused to speak Chinese all week?

I wondered why all the really important moments in parenting occur when we are hurrying. The hurry stopped. I sat down beside her and said, "Why, Jaclyn?" To which she replied, "I no like everybody look like Mama, nobody look like Jack-win." Then, after a pause, "I no like food at home," and, "In China, I understand what everybody saying," and more softly, "I no like share-ee Mama."

I had no idea what to say and was once again amazed at the way she could put her confused feelings into words.

"We can't stay here, Jaclyn," I said. "Mama doesn't understand what people are saying in China."

"*I* tell you," she said. Now the child who had refused to translate all week was ready to tell me what people were saying. Her message was clear: you be the one who looks different and can't understand everybody.

Then, finally, more softly yet, she disclosed the real source of her pain—she didn't want to leave Xiao Mei Mei. I told her, and felt more sure of it since I had found out he was registered for adoption, that Xiao Mei Mei would find a mama and come to America. She shook her head sadly; she was not convinced. After all, she saw for herself—he was still sitting in the same TV room where she had left him months ago. "But *I'm* his mama," she said in frustration. "Kids will hurt him. They take things from him. Nobody hug him. Nobody will say 'It OK' when he cry."

Finally, with my heart in my throat, I told her, "Jaclyn, you can come and live in China with Xiao Mei Mei when you are a big girl if you still want to. But now you are little and you need a mama. So you have to come home with me." And I knew as I said the words that if it ever came to that, I did love her enough to let her go. She seemed relieved and said with finality, "Yes, Xiao Mei Mei and I live in China when I big." With this compromise made, she was ready to get dressed and head back home.

She had such a pull of emotion. I still had the nagging doubt, as always, that maybe I didn't do the right thing when I removed her from her homeland.

After we boarded the plane, I closed my eyes and thought about the last few days. I realized that this trip had afforded me the opportunity to see my sister Laura in a new light. In our family she was the baby sister, and sometimes we still saw her that way. How wrong we were. She had a mother's heart, and that brought with it nerves of steel and the power of love. How blessed I felt to have a sister who could not sleep, who could not stem her tears, after seeing her child's orphanage. I had a strong inkling that she, too, would be back.

What a gift it had been to glimpse my brother-in-law in the most challenging emotional circumstances, the ones that give you insight into someone's real character. This glimpse had revealed a man of strength and faith. I thought of their generosity in attempting to adopt Jaclyn's best friend and how they had said, almost without stopping to think, that they had room in their small home and their hearts for Xiao Mei Mei. They were generous in a way that is rare. They did not give out of their abundance, but from their hearts.

I sighed with the relief that came with the knowledge that Jaclyn's baby was registered for adoption. I determined to find him a family as soon as we got home; it did not hurt to try. But the real prize was that we now not only knew the real name of Jaclyn's baby, but I also knew that Lou Jiao was Jaclyn's birth name. This piece of information in and of itself was worth the price of the trip.

We arrived home, and I walked in a fog of jet lag for several days. As Jaclyn helped me fold laundry one day, I said to her, "The next time we visit China, we will take the whole family so you can show your sisters where you used to live."

She began to cry. "I nebber want go back to China!" she said. "Please, Mama, say I nebber have to go back China again!" I was dumbfounded. Was this the same child who did not want to leave two days ago? When she was home, she felt as if she belonged here; when she was there, she felt as if she belonged there. But I always left China with a heavy heart. How could I expect that it would be any different for her?

Chapter Twelve

The "L" Word

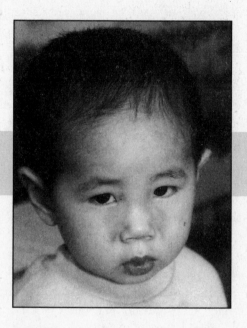

A boy is a magical creature . . . a freckle-faced, pint-sized, cat-chasing bundle of noise. But when you come home at night with only the shattered pieces of your hopes and dreams, he can mend them like new with two magic words—"Hi Dad."
—Alan Beck

*O*nce we arrived home, I was consumed with the guilt that came from seeing Xiao Mei Mei again. Jaclyn did not make it any easier. Each day she would find ways to weave his name into any topic, any discussion, any future plans. Her sadness was palpable. And, although I tried to hide it, my heart was heavy, too.

Finding a home for Jaclyn's baby was constantly on my mind. I began to write about Jaclyn and him and their unusual bond, and my stories were reprinted in some adoption forums. I secretly hoped that this would cause some other family, hopefully one that already had a dossier registered in China, to come forward and pledge to request him.

Jaclyn, too, had been deeply affected by our trip to China. Nearly every night since we had come home, she woke sobbing in her sleep. She was sure that the only issue preventing our adoption of Xiao Mei Mei was that there was no room in our home, so she carefully surveyed her domain.

She rejected her bed for him. "He might fall out, Mama!" she said. She then took me by the hand over to her sister's crib. She showed me one end of the bed and said, "Xiao Mei Mei," and then pointed to the other end and said, "Christ-ta-tee." She wasn't far off; he was so small he could practically have slept in a box.

Each night as bedtime approached, dread filled me. Listening to my children's prayers used to be a real highlight of the bedtime ritual for me. It tickled me to hear the personal nature of their requests; their lack of intimidation, and the things that they thought God needed to know about. My favorite from Kate was the night she ended her prayer by saying, "and give Jesus a big hug for me!" I thought that must have put a smile on God's face.

But Jaclyn's prayers for Xiao Mei Mei seemed to have taken on an even more frantic note. One night Jaclyn said this: "Dear God, Don't close the door! Xiao Mei Mei scared when the door closes. Now Xiao

Mei Mei sleep in one room and Jaclyn sleep in this-a room. [In China] Jaclyn and Mama see lots of kids and Xiao Mei Mei . . . but no mamas. Amen."

I could not understand how in the world God could stand to hear this child's pleas. But Jaclyn was steadfast in demonstrating the faith of a child. Jaclyn was sure that God heard her. I shared her prayers and some of the flavor of her desperation with my support group of adoptive moms. One said, "I think God can listen to Jaclyn's prayers because He knows you'll tell others about her experiences and then families will open their homes and their hearts to these kids. If I wasn't leaving on my own adoption journey next week, I would track him down and adopt him myself!"

But even after all my marketing efforts to find a home for Xiao Mei Mei, no one came forward. As days went by I became more and more discouraged. I had several inquiries, but in each case there was some obstacle: The wife was interested; the husband was not. The family already had another adoption in process. The family didn't have the financial resources.

I hung up the phone one early December evening from still another long phone call with a family that had some interest. Like a salesperson touting their wares, I went on and on with descriptors about how special Xiao Mei Mei was. The woman who called listened carefully and then said, "Maybe you should think about adopting him yourself. It sounds to me like you are the one who really loves him."

I swallowed hard. "My husband and I are not in a position to do another adoption now," I said lamely, floundering for an excuse. In a rush of words, I poured out all the rational reasons why we could not adopt this child. But my heart told me otherwise; I determinedly tried to ignore it.

I hung up the phone and called Andrea, my friend on the Great Wall staff.

"I haven't been able to find a family for Jaclyn's baby," I lamented. "What do you think his odds are of being matched to a family?" I knew Andrea would be honest with me, and she did not hedge in her reply.

"I don't know," she said sadly. "He will be three in a few months, and very few families are willing to take a risk on adopting the older kids. He is also a boy, and the overwhelming majority of families who adopt from China want girls. And I can't help but think of those pitiful pictures you showed me. Sometimes people refuse the referral of a child who appears so waiflike, so malnourished. They are afraid of the long-term effects on the child's health." Andrea sighed deeply and then said, "I don't think his chances are very good." I hung up with a knot in my stomach.

I didn't dare talk to Snow Wu, the director of the Great Wall adoption agency, about him. After all her extraordinary efforts to free Jaclyn from her entanglement in the system, including making her own trip to China to intercede with the officials, I didn't dare ask for a favor again from this lady that I so revered. I remembered our many conversations about Jaclyn and my endless nagging and figured she had heard enough from me to last a lifetime.

But unbeknownst to me, Ginny Heller, our friend Carl's wife and also an adoptive mom, was forwarding my writings about Jaclyn and her baby to Snow. One day I opened my email and got this incredible message from Snow: "I read this story about Jaclyn and her baby with many tears. If your family would like to adopt him, I will try to help. . . ."

I nearly gasped out loud. I couldn't believe it. After all she had done for us, I would never have been able to ask for her help again. But I didn't have to ask; she offered. Afraid to believe her words, I called her. "Snow, do you mean it? Do you think you could get Jaclyn's baby for our family?"

"I cannot promise you. You know I cannot. Identified adoptions are nearly impossible. I used many favors with the officials to bring Lou Jiao here. But if you want to try again, I will try. I will try my best. I will try my hardest for you as I do for all my families. But no promises," she said firmly.

I hung up the phone, and my mind began to race. If I could get together still another dossier, find a way to come up with the money, and not have my heart broken if the identified match, still a long shot, didn't occur, Snow would try. But I was still filled with nagging doubts.

My head told me this was an easy decision: just say no. I was a prag-matic thinker; adopting Jaclyn was the only decision I had made in my life without careful assessment of all the angles. After all, I had learned something in business school. So I pulled out a piece of paper and sat down to assess the pros and cons.

The reasons not to adopt him:

1. I'm not a good mom. I get bored after one game of Candy Land. I sweat at the kids' birthday parties until the clown gets there. I wanted to scream after reading *Goodnight Moon* three times. Kate coaches me before she lets me read to her class. I tried hard but lacked that knack for just being comfortable in kid world. Maybe this is because I have never been one myself. I was never meant to have so many kids; all my life I imagined myself as a mother of one. As a stretch. I went from childless and self-involved to being a mother of three, stepmother of three, and grandmother of two and a half [one daughter-in-law was preg-nant!] in a dizzying period of time. And I was just not good at it.

2. Boys—*ewww*! Didn't they love snakes and other wiggly things? Didn't they like to roughhouse and get dirty? Didn't they chew with their mouths open and snort milk through their noses? I lived in a house filled with sequined high heels and froufrou umbrellas (not mine). What kind of gender identity could a boy have in a home where Jaclyn claimed he would be her little sis-ter and where Barbie reigned, after they dressed him in bright pink sweaters and pink shoes at the orphanage? And how would I ever handle a teenage boy's adolescence? Girlie maga-zines and beer? Could I ever even say out loud the words *noc-turnal emission*? I didn't know anything about raising boys. I lived in girl world.

3. We owed more money than the national debt. At the moment we were living on an unsecured line of credit. We had done two

adoptions in one and a half years. Neither one was paid for. We had absolutely nowhere left to go for the money. We had two mortgages already. Our cars were both ready to die. I needed major dental work. Besides which, it was largely rumored in the school district that there would soon be a new administration. This meant I would soon be jobless, and I provided one-half of my family's income.

4. Which led me to my job. I was trying to make a difference, but what a price I was paying. This was the most incredibly stressful, hard, long-thankless-hours job I had ever had. And although I was deeply committed to it, I was never, ever not buried in work and not feeling guilty about all I still needed to do.

5. And when I was not at work, I was feeling the same about the home front. My kids needed more of me. When they fought over me, demanded I equalize things as I doled out every hug and kiss, I could almost feel the essence of my very soul seeping out. I thought sometimes of that awful scene in the movie *Jesus Christ Superstar* where Christ was walking down the street and a mob of hands was reaching for him, grabbing him, clamoring for him. I knew how that felt. I didn't have enough for the kids I had. And although anyone could have made a compelling argument for my need for therapy, I was currently holding it together on my own. Barely.

6. My condo was full. Really full. We had three bedrooms and three girls now and no yard. How in the world could we add a boy? Three girls in one room? Did anyone besides the Brady bunch ever attempt this and survive? Sometimes I thought that the bedroom doors were all that was standing between them and their complete annihilation of each other.

7. My house was trashed. Really trashed. I did at least one load of wash and ran the dishwasher once every day now and was still

always behind. I needed at least three weeks' notice for anyone to visit. I hyperventilated when friends said they wanted to "stop by." I had found myself actually hoping we could lose some of our friends so I didn't have to invite them over. You could stick to my kitchen floor, and that was on a good day . . . if you could actually make it to the kitchen.

8. Our ages. My husband was fifty-something. I was . . . well, suffice it to say we were not young. My husband wanted to retire someday . . . someday while he still could walk. He, being the eternal optimist, recently had a retirement estimate done. The report said: "You are $1,235,000 short of the funds you need to retire. You will not be able to save this amount in time to retire." We had put three kids through college and had three more to go.

9. I was tired. A week earlier I had the flu and had to lie in bed all day, aching, chilled, and nauseated, watching old movies on TV while chaos reigned outside. And then I realized it was one of the best days I'd had in a long time. I was really tired. Without lots of under-eye makeup, I had the scariest Halloween face on the block without a mask. And I was losing it. The night before, I had actually dug in the garbage to find an important check. And I found it there. While in the garage, I discovered a belt I had been looking for inside Kate's bike helmet. The state of my current life was not a pretty picture.

10. I made a solemn promise to Rick when we adopted Jaclyn that this was it. This was really it; we would not go back. And I meant it. We both knew that we couldn't save them all. For every "just one more child," there were still thousands left behind. It was funny how this argument seemed so rational in the abstract and so worthless in reality.

11. My to-do list was so long that I might die before it was all done. I had lost my day planner for half a day and, literally,

was frozen into nonfunctioning. It took me three years to find time to go to the dentist. And when I got there I found myself joyously anticipating the quiet of a few stolen moments in the waiting room; I was deeply disappointed that the dentist was on schedule. Every day was jam-packed. I was so busy doing, I didn't have time for living.

12. Fear. I was a coward. I was so paralyzed with fear during my first two adoptions that I was almost physically sick. Someone described the adoption trip as an "out-of-body experience"; I knew just what they meant. And this time I would not just have the what-in-the-world-am-I-doing fear but the older-child-and-all-the-baggage-they-may-have fear and the why-is-he-so-tiny—is-something-wrong fear and the he's-a-boy fear.

The reasons to adopt him:

1. Jaclyn loved him. She really loved him.

2. And so did I. It was liberating to finally say it out loud. I really loved this little guy.

3. I couldn't forget him. I tried to. I really did. I begged God to take away the haunting image of his face, but it was always there before me. And the feel of him, how could I ever forget the feel of him? So tiny. So sweet nestled in my arms.

4. Guilt. Could I ever survive the guilt of leaving him there? It cut into every joyful experience I had now. How could I ever say I didn't have room when I saw where he lived now? Every time I heard Jaclyn say, "I want him here with this-a mama," my heart tore a little more. And she said it every day.

Rick was as anguished as I was about what to do. Because we rarely had a chance to talk to each other at home without the kids interrupting, the discussion of what to do about Xiao Mei Mei now became the only topic of our brief phone conversations at work each day.

"Rick, do you think we have the patience for another child?" I asked. "I'm starting to think I only have the patience for two kids. And I didn't figure that out until we had three." He tried to laugh at my attempt at humor, but it came out as a strangled chortle instead.

"I know what you mean," he said sympathetically.

"I've tried praying about it. But I'm still clueless about what God wants us to do," I said. "In fact, I'm kind of hoping He'll tell you instead. Heard anything?" This time Rick didn't even attempt a laugh.

"I get irritated when I hear all your boy stereotypes," Rick said. "Don't forget that I raised two sons already. Yes, I'll concede that boys like snakes and snort milk through their noses and learn to burp the ABCs and make huge messes. But they also give big hugs and sloppy kisses and shout, 'Hey, Mom, I missed you today!' when they come home.

"I'm as worried as you are about the money thing," he went on. "But look at my family. I was one of six children raised in a house that was no more than eight hundred square feet, and we all turned out just fine. Kids don't need their own bedrooms and all the latest toys. What they need is family, love, support, and education. I think we might be able to manage that."

Jaclyn seemed to sense my weakening. As she readied for bed that night, she looked at the toilet and said, "In China, I hold Xiao Mei Mei over this-a one," as she pantomimed a trench-shaped hole in the ground. "Xiao Mei Mei fall in potty without me," she added sadly. Without her there, she was convinced that he was slipping on the wet floors, falling into the potty, scared at night, and having all his food stolen. She was good at stoking the guilt machine.

"Mama," she said, "how many kids can Mama get?" This was a source of continuing confusion for her; she asked it often, and none of my answers appeared to be satisfactory. I was puzzled by her interest in this, but knew how strict China was about the one-child-per-family policy and thought maybe Jaclyn knew something of it.

"Why are you asking, Jaclyn?" I said. She had evaded answering this before, but she now revealed the reason behind her question.

"When we go to my China, the teacher—not my teacher, different teacher—say to me, 'You family want Tan Dong Jin, not you.' I know family can only have one. I can't go get my baby or they keep me. You can just get one." She was in tears. Thinking back, I knew exactly when this had happened. There was a jovial worker there who I believe was just trying to joke with Jaclyn. Jaclyn liked to tease and has a good sense of humor. I could remember this lady talking to her, but of course I did not know what was said. I also remembered how Jaclyn shouted, "NO!" and buried herself in me, almost knocking Xiao Mei Mei from my lap.

"Jaclyn, that's not true," I said, trying not to show my distress over her secret fear. "You can adopt more than one child. That's how I got both you and Christy. I wouldn't allow you to be traded for Xiao Mei Mei."

"NO!" she said insistently. "Christ-ta-tee from *different* China. I nebber saw her before I come here. She not from *my* China." As much as I tried to clarify this, she thought of each orphanage as its own "China." She looked at me unconvinced; once she believed something, it was nearly impossible to dissuade her.

Jaclyn crawled into her bed, and I kneeled down next to it so she could begin to pray. "Dear God, Help Xiao Mei Mei! Help him find this-a mama. He no wear diaper; he go on little potty. Kids take his crackers, and I can't get the teacher. Get the teacher, God. Amen."

The potty reference was a cheap shot at her baby sister who was now, not very successfully, potty training. She liked to point out how much easier "her baby" would be to care for. I liked to note that she was as bossy in giving God directions as she was with everyone else. Then she looked at me and said, "I talk-a you, Mama," while turning my face directly to her and placing hers no more than three inches away. She meant business.

"Xiao Mei Mei want this-a mama, not go-away China mama."

"How do you know he wants this-a mama?" I asked.

"Because I tell him so!" She then continued, "On Saturday, put on a pretty dress. Daddy drive the car. Jaclyn, Katie, and Christ-ta-tee go to

Nana's house or Lola's or Willow's. Daddy and Mama go on *ee-po-ma* [airplane] to China to get Xiao Mei Mei. I can't go because you can only get one."

"Why do I have to wear a pretty dress?" I asked innocently, amused by her directives.

"Because you wear pretty dress when you get Jaclyn," she said with childish logic.

I went downstairs and burst into tears.

I agonized for weeks about what to do and continued to elicit advice from anyone who would listen. One day, an adoptive mom told me this: "Well, you've got some really great reasons for *not* doing it. They make sense. They sound logical and understandable. You've certainly thought it all out. But do you realize you have said the 'L' word?" I nodded in misery as she went on. "Love is a mighty powerful thing to fight. I have loved, been loved, and been in love. The one thing I know about love is that either it wins or you're miserable. There is no compromising love. There is no 'let's make a deal' with love. It wins or you lose. Love is not logical. Love doesn't care if boys like wiggly things. Love is not practical. Love doesn't care if you have the money or not. Love is not reasonable. Love doesn't care whether you have the time or the energy or not. Love doesn't care if you're already exhausted. It doesn't care who needs therapy. It doesn't care how full or dirty your house is. Love doesn't care if you are old or afraid. How can you fight love and hope to win?"

I'd heard the saying that sometimes God hits you so hard in the head that you need an aspirin. And that's exactly what happened. I had been so emotionally wrung out over the decision that I barely functioned. Rick was deeply torn, too.

"*If* we adopted him, what would we name him?" Rick asked one night as we pretended to watch television. I knew the "name game" was dangerous territory. Adoption experts say that once the child has a name, it's a sign that the parents have committed.

"Sam," I said without hesitation. Surprisingly, it was a name I had never felt any real attachment to before. "Samuel Edward. Edward for your grandfather." And although we played with a few other names (Jack? Too confusing with a child named Jaclyn already. Michael? No, it was ruined by knowing someone yucky with that name. Etc.), we were decided almost immediately.

"I like the fact that Samuel is a Biblical name," Rick said. "And it sounds enough like Xiao Mei Mei to make an easy sound transition." But the truth was, I had no idea how I *knew* this was the name with such certainty.

The next day Rick made the hour-long drive to visit his parents and ran this tenuous idea by them. It was our first time saying it out loud and waiting for the reactions.

"Dad, you know how fondly I still remember your father," Rick began as he sat on the overstuffed beige sofa in their tiny living room. "We've been thinking about adopting Jaclyn's baby, and if we do, we would like to use Edward as his middle name, after Grandpa. He seems like the perfect person to name this child after. I think about how he came to America all alone at age fourteen, how he determined to make a new life in a new land, how he worked in the coal mines for fifty years to support his family. I remember how short he was in stature, like Xiao Mei Mei, but what a giant he was in terms of what really mattered.

"Grandpa knew how to love with his whole heart," Rick said with a smile. "So we're thinking of the name Samuel Edward." Rick's father's eyes filled with tears. "Oh, son," he said, "you got them both right!" And then he showed him documents with Edward's official name: Eduardo Samuel Otto Desantis Champnella.

I had told Rick before I married him that there was only one reason I wanted to marry him: because I simply couldn't imagine my life without him. And this was how our family now felt about Xiao Mei Mei: we simply couldn't imagine our lives without him. So we decided to go for it. We would start the paperwork and make it clear that we were asking only for him; no other child would be acceptable. This was about this child, not just any child. We determined, too, to remember that the goal here was to find him a family. If he was referred to another home, we promised ourselves that we would swallow hard and dry our tears. Then we would fervently try to find his new family and open our arms, our hearts, and our circle of love to include them, to make them part of our own family. We trusted that God would know our hearts as he knew Jaclyn's. And that he would make the perfect plan for Xiao Mei Mei. And for us.

Chapter Thirteen

The Twist in the Road

Love is the condition in which the happiness of another person
is essential to your own.
—Robert A. Heinlein

B ut *life rarely goes according to our* plans. I called Andrea at Great Wall late one afternoon. "We're going to go for it," I said. "We've decided to start the paperwork for Jaclyn's baby. We love him too much to leave him there. And I know Snow is a miracle worker; if she says she will help get him for our family, I believe that she will." Andrea was happy about our decision.

A few hours later the phone rang. It was Andrea.

"I don't know how to explain this," she began. "But two hours after you called, your sister Laura called. And she said the exact same thing. She said that they have decided to adopt Xiao Mei Mei." And then she chuckled at the irony. "I think that you need to talk to each other and sort this all out. Let us know what you decide."

I could hardly wait to talk to Rick. He got home late, stuck in heavy traffic that had been stymied by a blizzard. I told him we had to talk, and he followed me into the bedroom. I shut the door so we could have privacy from our three little eavesdroppers. When I told Rick what had happened, he looked as if the wind had been knocked out of him. He began to pace furiously, unsure what to do to resolve things. He ran his hands through his hair and furrowed his brow in frustration.

"We need to get them on the phone right away! He's ours! He's *Jaclyn's* baby," he said with agitation. It was a weeknight and too late to drive over there to talk in person. I dialed the phone and clutched it tightly. Laura answered; we started out as the respective spokespersons for our teams.

"Laura," I began, "Rick and I decided to adopt Jaclyn's baby. Andrea just called and said you called Great Wall today, too, and said the same thing." I took a breath and let her respond.

"Don't you remember that Jeff and I said we wanted to adopt him?" she said. "We've wanted to do it all along. The only reason we didn't start a dossier as soon as we got back from China was because of Julie's dismal assessment of our chances. But if Snow has promised to help you, certainly she would help us, too." Laura was right about this; she had said that she wanted to adopt him first. But this was not a childhood squabble over who "called it" first; now the stakes were much higher.

"Are you sure, Laura?" I asked.

"I'm sure," she said. "I'm as sure about this as I have been about anything in my life. We love him."

"We love him, too," I said weakly. I knew this criterion wouldn't put us any closer to making a decision. It was impossible to gauge who loved him most. "I remember what you went through when you lost the referral of Jin Xun Li; your heart was broken. You of all people know how difficult identified adoptions are to do, how uncertain they are. Are you going to be able to stand going through all that again? What if he's referred to another family? Have you thought about how you would deal with that?"

"I know that won't happen again," she said. "I just know it won't. I know this doesn't make sense, but I have a strong feeling that things will work out this time."

Seeing that we were going nowhere, Jeff picked up the receiver on an extension. Rick stood behind me, still pacing the floor, too anxious, too emotional, too afraid of saying the wrong thing and unintentionally hurting either of them to get on the phone.

"What about the money? Where are you going to get the money for another adoption, Laura?" I said gently.

"Where are *you*?" she retorted. We were about even on this score. Their family budget was stretched to the limit; there was no room for extras. But we were heavily in debt and had two adoptions that were not yet paid for.

"Andrea told me that one of the factors the Chinese consider most strongly is family income," I said, trying hard not to offend. "Because we both work, she thinks this will increase our chances."

"But if you adopt him, he'll be in day care all day," Laura said. "I'm home already with the kids. What's one more?" She, too, was trying to dance gently around my feelings. "Besides, don't you think that a boy needs a dad who wants to coach Little League? Rick has already raised two sons, but Jeff's never had a chance." She left implied, but unsaid, the fact that Jeff was also twenty years younger than Rick.

I had a strange déjà vu moment. Back in college, when my friends and I were feeling crabby we played a game that we called "Who has the worst life?" Each person got to list all the reasons why their life, at the moment, was the worst, and we collectively voted on the winner—or maybe we should have dubbed them the loser—of the contest. That person got our collective sympathy, and the rest of us felt better because we didn't have it so bad in comparison. This conversation was beginning to remind me of the reverse of that game. We were each trying to point out what we had to offer that the other did not.

"I hadn't even considered that you might still be interested in adopting him. I know you're still in the throes of Willow's adjustments. I know how frustrated you've been by her strong will and the endless battles. I know how full your house and your life are. You seem so exhausted all the time. Are you sure that you want a fourth child when you have three children under age four now?" I thought of all the reasons not to do it that I had on my list; she had all the same obstacles and maybe even more.

The stacks were even. Neither side was budging.

"But you have three small children, too," she protested. "You're busy and stressed, too. Besides, Jeff and I had always planned to adopt another child someday. You and Rick said you were done." She was right about this.

Then Jeff hit a home run by saying with a chuckle, "Look, our three children together plus Xiao Mei Mei doesn't equal the effort and energy required to raise one Jaclyn." Hmmm . . . it was hard to refute that one. We all knew it was true.

Although Laura and I have common blood between us, our differences are such that it's sometimes hard to believe we are sisters. I had approached this issue by taking inventory of my life and seeing all that I didn't have to offer: time, patience, money, space, and energy. My sister had inventoried her life and saw what she did have to offer: faith, love, and family. And she realized that those things were huge. Next to that, I felt very small. So I conceded; she would be the "champion mother." I would be the aunt.

But we had both come to realize that we had champion husbands. Men that didn't care a hoot if their son came from their gene pool. Men that would be proud to call the smallest kid on the playground their son. Men who understood that the measure of a man has nothing to do with stature.

"We'll share him," Laura offered. "You know we'll share him with you. We live so close, he can visit Jaclyn whenever she wants."

"Laura, we have to agree that we will put our collective effort into this," I said. "It's too important to Jaclyn. We have to pledge that we will accept any help, including money if we need it, that we will do the paperwork as a team, that we will beg if we have to, that we will do whatever we need to do to bring Jaclyn's baby home to our family." I realized that in committing together to this child, we were, more than ever before, one family.

I couldn't meet Rick's eyes when I hung up the phone. He shot me a look of utter betrayal. "Laura said she felt sick, literally sick to her stomach when she thought of him going to any home but hers," I said as a way to justify my concession. "She's my little *sister*. I could never let her hurt like that. I know how much she loves him, too." Rick nodded mutely, afraid to trust his voice. He walked away with his head down. The decision was made.

And so, his name would not be Samuel. Amazingly, my sister and members of her husband's family shared the same middle name: Lee. And even though they could not share their blood with this child, they wanted to share with him a part of both of them. His name would be Lee. His middle name would be Mitchell in honor of the only real hero in our family, Colonel Mitchell. He was a leader among men in the Civil War. A man to be reckoned with. A brave man. We hoped that this name would somehow instill courage in our little hero.

One of my friends said, upon hearing the name, "I don't care what you name him; I'm going to call him blessed. Here's a child who didn't have anyone, who now has two families clamoring for him."

When we were in China I had begged Jaclyn to tell Xiao Mei Mei that we were working to find him a home and a mama. She adamantly refused. She herself had been a victim of that endless waiting for too long. She did not want him to suffer from empty hopelessness. Now he had reason to hope. So now we prayed that God would find us worthy of Jaclyn's baby. And that he would forgive us our fears and doubts.

"Please, God, bring Jaclyn's baby home to us." This would become our mantra, as it had been hers for so long. And I desperately hoped we would not be too late.

We purposefully avoided telling Jaclyn about the plans to adopt Xiao Mei Mei. We just couldn't handle her disappointment, along with our own, if it didn't happen. But she was very intuitive, and sometimes I thought she could see into my very soul. The next night she came to me and, for the first time, said, "Mama, I *will* see Xiao Mei Mei again." She said it with such peace and certainty it took my breath away.

I looked into her eyes and silently thanked her. I thanked Jaclyn for making us love her baby. I thanked her for once again showing us the way.

Chapter Fourteen

The Lessons Learned at Chinese School

The strongest oak tree of the forest is not the one that is protected from the storm
and hidden from the sun. It's the one that stands in the open where it is
compelled to struggle for its existence against the winds and the rains
and the scorching sun.
—Napoleon Hill

*J*aclyn *continued her Saturday attendance* at Chinese school, and as time went by I began to wonder who was learning more from this experience—she or I. While she was busy trying to retain her Chinese, I was learning what it was like for people who leave their homelands to live in a strange new culture. I was the only parent there, out of about three hundred, who did not know Chinese. I was the one who couldn't read the posted bulletins. I was the one who didn't understand the public address announcements. I was the one who couldn't stand around and join in the animated chatter of the other parents. I was the one who couldn't read the notices that were sent home. I was the one who brought her child on the wrong day because I did not understand the schedule. I was the one who did not know to dress her child in a costume for the party. I was the one who looked different.

The other parents tried to help me while sometimes attempting to hide their looks of embarrassment at my mistakes. Most of the moms seemed to have only one child, and they sat at the back of the room through the entire class. I didn't have this luxury since I had two other children to care for. So Lily's mom made sure Jaclyn made the class change successfully. And another mom sometimes tried to help me understand the public address announcements.

Jaclyn took a traditional Chinese dance class there. While dance class was going on, the moms were busy doing some type of beautiful Chinese needlework on the dance scarves. They had given me my assignment—a green scarf—and all the materials I needed to "make it." I had absolutely no idea what I was to do. They giggled as they patiently tried to show me. I was considering stapling the sequins on it.

They helpfully gave me some information about where to get Jaclyn's dance costume, since it was clear I would not be able to make it myself—I had not yet satisfactorily completed my scarf assignment. The information was all in Chinese; again I had no idea what I was to do.

Then the dance teacher cornered me. "Jaclyn cannot dance," she told me firmly in broken English. "You must have her show you dance at home."

Then she glanced at me and rightly concluded that I did not know traditional Chinese dance. "If she cannot do it, I don't know what to do . . . ," she said with a sigh and thinly disguised exasperation at my deficiencies.

When it was time for the performance, Jaclyn let me know I had deficiencies in her eyes, too. As I struggled with her hair, barely two inches long and refusing to go into the designated style, she pulled impatiently away.

"I want a China mama fix my hair," she said in annoyance at my attempts. Lily's mom, hearing the fuss, gladly took over. I was defeated.

The next week, her pretty, young classroom teacher said she must speak to me. "Do you understand that Jaclyn has homework every week?" she asked me, talking with exaggerated slowness as if addressing the seriously feebleminded.

"Yes," I stammered in reply. Then, trying to excuse my negligence I offered, "But I can't read it. I don't know what she is to do." Several pages came home each week, and, although I puzzled over them, I had absolutely no idea what the assignments were.

"This is very bad problem," the teacher said to me seriously. "Don't you understand that homework is very important to learning?"

I was an administrator in a public school system. I was mortified.

I talked about all this with a friend who then related a similar experience she had. Several years ago, she had volunteered with another mom who had just arrived in America to be "room mothers" for her daughter's class. Although this woman's heart was in the right place, due to language barriers she generally did not understand what was expected of her. At the end of the year, she wrote my friend a note thanking her for understanding "when she had no brain" and for helping her be a part of things.

Now I was the one "with no brain." And this small taste of what life was like for all those who chose to bravely leave a land whose traditions they know, whose language they spoke and understood, whose people they could blend in with, left me in awe of that kind of courage. It was hard to be different. Even for a few hours each week.

And then I looked at my own school district. How many times did we send home notes written in a language that a parent couldn't understand? How many times did we speak to them with exaggerated slowness and thinly disguised frustration? How it must hurt those who only want to help their children, just as I don't want to fail Jaclyn.

And to think that when I enrolled her in this school, I thought all the lessons would be hers.

While we tried to celebrate Jaclyn's heritage, her past surfaced in painful ways, too. Late one night, exhausted, I put on my pajamas early and climbed into bed with the newspaper. Rick had a late meeting at work, and Kate and Christy had fallen asleep early watching a video. I heard the patter of feet coming down the stairs and knew before I saw her face that it was Jaclyn. She still fought sleep. I would find her sometimes lying awake in her bed hours after the other girls had fallen asleep.

Jaclyn walked over to my bureau, where I had a framed picture of her referral photo, the photo that I had first seen on the Internet. There was nothing extraordinary about her face in the photo, but the look in her eyes was haunting; they projected such sadness, such longing, such confusion, and so much pain. When I had locked eyes with those in that picture, my heart had immediately told me that she was mine.

As I watched her study the photo, I remembered back to the day I first met Jaclyn. She approached me with an identical expression on her face and that same pain in her eyes. She was immediately recognizable as "the little girl in the green coat." She was immediately recognizable as mine.

I later received letters from people all over the United States who told me stories about how they, too, had seen her photo on the Internet and how that picture, that look, in some way touched their hearts or influenced their decision to adopt.

Jaclyn had seen this picture many times. Now she brought it over to me, perched on the edge of the bed, and said, "After I there long time [presumably after the required waiting period] they come to me. They say, 'You mama *never, ever* come back for you.'" Jaclyn paused in her rendition of the story to compose herself and to make sure I understood the significance of that pronouncement.

She then bravely went on, "They take me downstairs where they make the picture. They tole me, 'We take your picture to help try to find you new mama.'" She paused again. "That mama *you*," she said, pointing at me with a smile.

I smiled back weakly. How in the world could anyone have told a horrific reality like that to a two-and-a-half-year-old child? After living with her for so long and hearing so much else about her life, I should not have been surprised by now that she could recall it so vividly. It was as if she remembered the words so clearly, so precisely, because of the searing impact they had left upon her little heart. Somewhere inside her, all the hurt, all the pain, was stored, as if she had inventoried her past and locked it away. And I didn't know how to get to that place inside her so that I could help her heal; maybe I was foolish to think it could ever heal.

But her eyes, then and now, betrayed it all. But even this did not prepare me for what was to come next.

It was a freezing winter night, and Jaclyn asked if she could climb into bed with me. I lifted the covers and she crawled in, content to lie next to me while I read in the dim pool of light cast by the small bedside lamp.

I thought she might fall asleep, but she was wired. This was a night when the demons were out in full force. Jaclyn showed me that she had a very small hole in her pajamas. She seemed agitated; way out of proportion to what would be a normal reaction to such a small problem. She struggled for the right word and then used some very detailed pantomime to ask me if a rat had bitten a hole in her pajamas while she was sleeping. I reassured her that this was not what had happened, but silently wondered if this was why she did not like having a bed that was so close to the ground. In her orphanage, the children's beds had been very high off the ground.

"Mama, they [rats] come out when it dark. Teacher close the door to make them stay out. But they come in. Teacher chase them and hit them like this"—she demonstrated a hitting motion with a stick. She shuddered, as if sickened by the memory. Jaclyn was, not coincidentally, deathly afraid of all small animals.

When she told me this, all I could think of was all the children in this world who lived in places where most Americans would not be caught dead. And she was undisputedly from one of the best orphanages in China.

Her eyes were bright and she studied my face intently before she decided to trust me with this: "When I live in my China," she said, "the teachers make me do this." With that she got out of bed and stood with her arms stretched shoulder level at her sides. "I have to stand like this a long, long time. I hurt very, very bad. The sun very, very hot," she said, her eyes moist with tears at the memory.

"I make too much noise," she said as an explanation for this punishment. She searched my face intently, deciding whether to continue or to close down.

Oh, God, I pleaded, how can there be more than what she has already told me? I wanted to cover my ears. I wanted to scream. I wanted to hide. Please, God, please don't let this be true. But I knew it was. Somebody hurt my daughter. My Jaclyn. My baby. The knowledge of the truth of her disclosure reverberated through my body, the same phrase over and over: somebody hurt my baby. I put on my good-mother mask. I swallowed my tears, my rage, and my ache. And she went on.

"Water come down from my head," she said as she indicated how sweat formed on her face. "But I not allowed to wipe it. It get so hot, hot, hot in the sun. I so hot and thirsty, but I not allowed to drink. I have to stand like this a very long, long time." She began to get agitated at the memory.

"Mama," she said, "it hurt very, very bad."

And there was more. She did not know the word for *stick*, so she got a picture of a balloon and showed me the stick it was tied to. "This-a one," she said. "They hit me with this-a one." And she demonstrated how they slashed her back repeatedly as she counted out loud.

And there was more. "This-a one make bad boo-boos on me. I all red." She stopped again to compose herself. "Mama," she said again, "I hurt very, very bad."

"Who did this to you, Jaclyn?" I asked, almost unwilling to believe that the staff I had met could do such a thing. She went into the great room and retrieved the blue photo album that contained the pictures of our trip. She laid it on the bed so that we could look at the pictures together. I was relieved to see that it was not the one she called "the school teacher" that I loved so. I was relieved it was not the gentle assistant director that I loved so. It was not one of those I believed to be special.

But there was more. She told me all the names of the children who were "naughty" and it seemed were beaten the most. She included the names of children that she loved.

"But I not let them hit my baby," she said proudly. "He not naughty," she told me. "They only hit him one time."

"What did he do, Jaclyn?" I asked, not sure I wanted to know the answer.

"He not move away from Jaclyn. They tell him to move but he not go," she said.

"But Mama," she assured me, "I hold him when he *cruela*. I rock him. I tell him, 'It OK.' I wipe his tears off." She thought about this and was silent. And then she added softly, "No one hold me when I *cruela*." And then, more softly, with a distant look in her eyes, "I no have a mama."

My mind knew and understood that it was different there. My rational mind knew that they were understaffed, resources were meager, and that there were many, many children. I knew from my own experience how really difficult and stubborn Jaclyn could be. I knew that not everyone felt as I did about the wrongness of hitting children. And yet, when I thought of it . . . somebody hurt my baby.

And the deepest pain of all? A child who knew how to comfort when she was not comforted herself. A child who cried without a mama's love to protect her. A child who knew that her baby was still there.

"Don't tell Daddy," she made me promise. She trusted only me with her secrets. Even after all my assurances, she was ashamed. And I, too, was ashamed . . . deeply ashamed that I didn't do more . . . deeply ashamed that this was the world my Jaclyn knew.

Chapter Fifteen

The Ever-Present Xiao Mei Mei

All the day
I held the memory of you . . .
And sowed the sky with tiny clouds of love. . . .
—Rupert Brooke

One morning as I began clearing the breakfast dishes, Jaclyn turned to me with a winsome smile.

"Mama, I have *an idea*," she said with feigned brightness. I was always surprised when I heard Jaclyn use a new word for the first time. The amazing thing was that she almost always used it correctly. I had never heard her use this word before, and I wondered if she understood what it meant.

"We need one more in this-a house. If Xiao Mei Mei come here, he could sleep in my bed with me. And Christ-ta-tee sleep in little bed." I was silent at this, the hundredth plan she had proposed about how to make room for her baby. I still did not comment about the adoption plans for him, knowing that if they failed, the depths of her grief would be like a bottomless well. She listened to my silence, then launched into plan B.

"Mama, I have an idea!" she said again with enthusiasm. "Willow [my bachelorette sister] no have a baby. Willow need a baby to hold! Xiao Mei Mei need somebody hold him at night." *A perfect match!* her delighted smile said. With new energy she continued on, "Willow get a little chair with a seat belt like Christ-ta-tee have. He not get carsick. He a good baby."

She had inventoried what was missing at Willow's house and anticipated what Willow would need to be a satisfactory mom. I was sure that Jaclyn, herself the queen of car sickness, had no idea if her baby got carsick, but she was always marketing his goodness. And she seemed to wonder why these obvious matches were apparent only to her.

Jaclyn's baby was on my mind constantly, too. I had noticed that all Jaclyn's joy in her new life existed beneath the shadow of longing. There was a certain day in January on which I, too, could not contain my longing for Jaclyn's baby. Unable to communicate with him directly in any way and sure that the feelings inside me would not stop overflowing into tears unless I somehow got them out, I sat down and wrote him a letter:

> *Dear Xiao Mei Mei,*
>
> *As I write this, I am sitting here with the heavy heart that comes from the realization that today, January 17, is your birthday. When I told Jaclyn today was your birthday, she began to cry. She knows what it is to have a birthday in her new life and that all of it will be denied you. Is there any recognition at all of this momentous day of yours, sweet boy? Jaclyn tells me that there is no such thing as "Happy Birthday" in China, and I know she is a witness to the truth of your life there. I know that there is no cake with candles on it to mark this special day. I know that there are no presents wrapped in shiny gift wrap with your name on them. I know that there are no streamers and balloons. I know that there are no excited friends playing games and singing "Happy Birthday" in your honor. Next year, I promise you, there will be balloons. . . .*
>
> *You have now lived in the orphanage for exactly thirteen months. Of course, I realize that there is no way to know what day is really the anniversary of your birth. There is only one who holds that knowledge deep in her heart. And, although I like to believe that all births are cause for celebration, there is no way to know if your birth was a day of happiness or of sorrow. Today I will say a prayer for your birth mother and her grief. I know she remembers you on the day of your birth and I suspect every other day, too. And I'll pray, too, that you will someday know a world in which a mother's will prevails over impossible options thrust upon her by others.*
>
> *If you only knew how knowing you has touched my heart and that of so many others. Even when Jaclyn had no words to communicate with me, her love for you was the first thing she tried to make me understand. When we first adopted her she carefully pointed you out in every photo and called you by her pet name for you. When she awoke, profoundly sad each morning, your pictures were the first things she looked for; she studied them with such a heavy heart.*
>
> *On her first full day as my daughter, I sorted out the piles of*

clothes we had brought for the orphanage. Although she could not have understood what I was doing, she quickly culled from the pile all the tiniest outfits and showed them to me and said your name over and over as she put them into a neat pile for you.

Jaclyn chattered about you nonstop to our guide so that this woman, who could understand her, would convey to us her pride in her care for you. She told us then that she had given you "all her love," and even before she said it in words, it was obvious. She delighted in telling little anecdotes about cute and amusing things you had done, and she told them with the same pride that a mother has for her darling baby. And once Jaclyn could communicate with us directly, she clarified for us that you were, indeed, "her baby."

I'll never forget the first time we met, how Jaclyn ran over to scrutinize your dress and gently fix your pant leg and how she fussed over your tiny shirt. You locked your sad little eyes on hers and desperately held on to her hand. Even when you got pushed aside in the excited throng of children, Jaclyn found you and reclaimed your little hand again. And then when she had to go, your silent tears began as she gently rocked and comforted you. I know how alone and sad you must have felt that day, sweet boy. Her newfound family separated you from the "child mother" she had become to you; her joy became your sorrow.

I received a note from another mother of an older child in your orphanage who told me that her daughter also loved you and, like Jaclyn, sneaked you food at night and loved to hold you. She told me this to try to ease my heart by saying, "Just think, if our daughters both loved him so, maybe there is some other special little girl there now who loves him, too, and is watching over him."

Maybe there is, but I know there is no one who could love you as fiercely as Jaclyn. Living with her has been like living with a very short mother who has had her baby wrenched from her arms. You are never far from her thoughts; thoughts of you permeate both times of joy and times of sorrow in this house.

We never know when memories of you will surface. When we had a special holiday prayer on Christmas, Jaclyn's prayer was for a mama for you. When Jaclyn was so sick with the flu that she could barely speak without chills making her teeth chatter, she still squeaked out a prayer for you. I have come to realize that Jaclyn asks God for nothing for herself, but all her prayers contain pleas for a mama for you.

And so, dear child, you have now invaded my heart. You were once just another nameless, faceless, familyless child in a myriad of lost children. Your picture was not in anyone's family album. Now your picture is in mine. It also sits on my dresser and on my mantel and belongs in that place as rightfully as the pictures of my other children. And I know of three other households that display your picture with their family photos, too.

Your story, as told by Jaclyn, has touched so many others that funds are now accumulating to pay for your journey home. I already have a box of special gifts, given with great love and hopefulness, awaiting your arrival.

I was almost as anxious as Jaclyn to see you again when we visited in October. I had not held you the first time; that privilege belonged only to Jaclyn. But this time she wanted to share you. She is very wise, and I know she held herself back so that my sister and I could feel the sweetness of you for ourselves. Jaclyn was dismayed to see your shoes on the wrong feet, but she wanted me to fix them, for me to be "the mama" this time, not her. Her pain at seeing you sitting in the same spot where she left you was almost too much to bear. And when she sneaked back around the corner after she had bid you good-bye and saw your silent tears, she turned and ran with a look in her eyes that spoke of the deepest grief imaginable. Because of you, she did not want to leave China.

This birthday, your third, marks the day in the world of adoption that you go from being a possibly adoptable toddler to a child with suddenly fewer options. After age three, the adoption experts tell me, potential parents are afraid that you will have been too deeply scarred by your past to become whole again. Luckily, there are many others like me that know a different truth. Don't give up hope, little guy; your mama is coming for you.

As much as you may believe that Jaclyn abandoned you in the

same way that your birth mother did, I am here to tell you that she did not. Not even for a day. She has made so many others love you, pray for you, hope for you, and care about you that there is now a powerful wave of love washing you home. And I fervently pray that your homecoming will be to our extended family.

I feel like a fool for not understanding that you belonged here sooner. How I regret not starting adoption proceedings myself to bring you home months ago. I foolishly thought that a small child would get over her devotion to you. That was before I knew Jaclyn. That was before I really understood the depth of her love for you.

When she had lost everything and everyone that she held dear, and almost at the same time her second adoption fell through, you arrived at the orphanage. You became the one that she transferred all her feelings to. Her love for you kept her heart intact. She needed to love you as much as you needed her love. Thank you for that. Had she not had the responsibility for your care, I am not sure what would have happened to her. If she had not had you to hold on to, to give her life a greater purpose, I am not sure who she would have become. It certainly would have been someone remarkably different from the incredibly loving child that she is.

You could not have found a more devoted protector. She has been like a beacon illuminating my understanding of the life that holds you. She will not forget. So, dear child, as you live this day in the never-ending routine of sorrow that surrounds you, hang on to hope. Because next year, I promise you, there will be balloons.

Happy Birthday, dear Xiao Mei Mei! I celebrate your life, and those of all you have touched.

Love,

Cindy (aka Jaclyn's mom and your second biggest fan)

Chapter Sixteen

Jaclyn's Past

Our lives begin to end the day we become silent about things that matter.
—Martin Luther King, Jr.

*I*n *bits and pieces that came out at* all times, but mostly at bedtime when all the monsters came out of hiding, Jaclyn told me about her former life. I was amazed at the clarity of her recollections. They were mostly of isolated events, many of them traumatic. Some events she recounted many times in exactly the same way. And just when I thought I had heard it all, new bits of information would come forth.

Not surprisingly, her mother was the first in this cast of characters that she chose to tell me about. We were sitting in the pediatrician's office waiting for Jaclyn's next set of inoculations. She had already had one series, so she knew what was ahead. She was frightened, and as the long moments passed until the nurse appeared with the designated shots, I could see her visibly trembling under the thin cotton gown. I tried to distract her by reading to her, but she did not have much interest in books. Her eyes were filled with fear, and this triggered her memory.

"My China mama no want me. She tell me she no want me. She take me on pur-dee horse. I wait and wait. She no come back. I no want go-away China mama," she began. And then, the pitch of her voice increasing with her anger, she said, "She no give me something to eat. She no give me breakfast. I hungry all the time."

It had never occurred to me that a child so young would remember her birth family. I was now almost used to her renderings of her life in the institution. My ache over her past was now so constant that I no longer winced sharply at new revelations. Unsure of what to say, I tried to defend her mother in hopes of dissipating some of Jaclyn's anger.

"Maybe there was no food at all, Jaclyn," I said gently. "Maybe she was poor and didn't have any food." Jaclyn, who now lived in the land of plenty, wasn't buying it. She knew that a mama protected you from all the bad in the world; she believed that hers had failed.

"Did your mama eat breakfast?" I questioned, certain that there was no mother alive who would let her child starve while she herself ate.

"No," Jaclyn said, refusing to see the connection between this and the lack of food. And then, curious myself about this significant person from her past, I asked, "What did she look like, Jaclyn? Can you remember what she looked like?"

"She have glasses like Nana. Her hair like this," Jaclyn said, indicating with her fingers hair that was shoulder length. "Her face yucky." Jaclyn waved her hands dismissively, and it was apparent that this last remark arose from her hurt and anger. "I NOT love her. I only love this-a mama. I no want go-away mama."

"Jaclyn," I said gently, "it's OK to love us both. Mama will always love you. You can love your China mama, too." Jaclyn looked at me intently. "Maybe your China mama couldn't take care of you. Maybe she didn't have enough food or money. Maybe that's why she had to go away." It was clear from her look that Jaclyn didn't accept this. We sat in silence, and I was almost relieved when the nurse appeared.

Jaclyn wanted to share with me the hard-won wisdom that had come as a result of her troubled past. Later in the week, Kate said, "Mama, where's Nana? We haven't seen her or talked to her in such a long time." My mother takes a few extended vacations each year and is generally incommunicado during these absences. Although my mind understood that she should be allowed these lapses from mothering—after all, her children are all middle-aged—my heart missed her desperately when she was gone.

"She's in Florida, Kate, for a whole month. I really miss her."

Jaclyn was busy eavesdropping, as was her practice. Afterward she got me aside and looked into my eyes very seriously while making this startling pronouncement, "You got go-away mama." She paused to let the significance of this settle in. Then she continued with this advice, "You need get two mamas."

I chuckled to myself at her heads-up and was glad when my "go-away mama" returned a week later so I didn't have to replace her.

A few weeks later as we were coming home from school, Jaclyn had another bout of car sickness. After we turned into the driveway, I held her head while she tried hard not to be sick. As she regained her color, I was surprised to hear her say, "I no like car. I like bicycle." Jaclyn had only recently ridden a bicycle for the first time, so I was intrigued by where this had come from.

"Did you ride on a bicycle before?" I asked her.

"My grandma. She take me on bicycle. I have little seat on back of the bike. She take me to her house when my mama go to work. It not far." Another character from her past had arrived.

"What did you do there?" I asked.

"She wash-ee me. She watch me while my mama at work," Jaclyn said.

"Did you play? Were there any other children to play with?" I asked.

"I no play. There no toys in China." She said this as though this reality should have sunk into my head by now.

"What can you remember about your grandma, Jaclyn?" I asked.

"I have two grandmas, but mostly just see one. Her name Nee-nee." I found out later that this is the word for paternal grandmother in Chinese. "She wear glasses like Nana, too."

A few weeks later, Jaclyn was tenderly putting a Band-Aid on an imaginary injury that Christy had sustained. She soothed her gently while she did so and then told me, "I have a baby sister in China." Another piece of the puzzle. I wondered if this was where she first learned baby care so that she could take such good care of her Xiao Mei Mei.

"Tell me about your sister, Jaclyn," I said. "Do you remember her name?"

Jaclyn shook her head in frustration as the name eluded her.

"She not go with me to my grandma house. She stay with my China mama," Jaclyn said. "She sleep by my China mama by her bed. Jackwin sleep in other room on couch with little blanket. She drink from this one"—and with that Jaclyn indicated my breast—"but she hungry, too, all the time. She cry and cry." Jaclyn thought about this and then added with pride in her voice, "My baby sister like me."

Jaclyn was not as forthcoming about her father. There were two men in the shadows of her past; apparently the two girls had different fathers. The baby sister did not go with Jaclyn to Grandmother's house, which fits with the girls having different fathers. Jaclyn knew which one her father was. "He had a scary hat[mask] like a lion. He scare me at bedtime. He scary." She said her parents were not married, but Jaclyn used the word *marry* to refer to any happy social event between a man and a woman. If my husband and I were going out to a dress-up event, she called that a "marry." I suspected that what she meant was that they did not have happy interactions together.

Once Jaclyn saw on the TV news a man covered with tattoos. "My China daddy have those," she said. She later showed us where the three tattoos were located on his arms and shoulders.

Some of the interactions between Jaclyn's grandmother and her father were terrifying to her. She vividly remembered a dispute between them that she believed arose out of her potty training. I thought with a chuckle that some parental struggles must be universal; this is certainly an area where parents I knew had lost it, too. However it began, this argument escalated into a violent dispute. Jaclyn says that her grandmother "hit him on the hand with glass. His finger get like an apple" (meaning that it turned red). I presumed from her accompanying hand gestures that blood was also involved. The exchange was very frightening, and she recounted it often.

Other events she recalled with specificity, too. One night as Jaclyn struggled to fall sleep, she begged me to come and lie down with her. Wearily, I did, and it was on this night that I first heard her version of her abandonment:

"My mama take me on a pur-dee horse. My mama tole me she no want me. I wait and wait for her to come back. She no come back." From what I had already learned from the orphanage officials, it seemed as if she was left in a forest, and it was a miracle that she was discovered. No one knew how long she had been there before she was found. I wasn't sure I was prepared to hear the answer to this question, but asked it anyway.

"Can you remember that time when you were lost, Jaclyn? Can you remember what happened?"

"I not *lost*," she said emphatically. "I wait for my mama to come back. I sit there and wait and wait, but she not come back."

The time period that she waited would be hard to even guess about. She never spoke of it again. I could only imagine the horror of it. Was she cold? Hungry? Thirsty? How many nights did she wait? Is this where her terror of the dark was born? Are the scars on her face the result of tree branches as she wandered in the woods? She was only two and a half at the time. In many ways I was glad she did not recite the full horror of her experience. Maybe her mind had granted her a small kindness by blocking this one memory that was too horrific to recall. Maybe she remembered and could not bear to share it. Maybe she wanted to save me this pain.

"Another mama find me. I all dirty. She take me home and wash-ee me. They take me and give me this-a one bag of water. It goes through this-a one [makes hand gestures like long tubing] into my hand. It hurt, but I don't move my hand. They give me two bags of water. I too sick to eat rice. They give me baby rice." I was amazed at the accuracy of her description of an IV tube feeding. The fact that she received this type of medical care, rare in China, indicated that she was very dehydrated and sick when she was found.

I knew that she somehow ended up with a policeman who brought her to the orphanage. But from her accounts, she had the clear expectation that her mama would come back to get her. Then the day came when "they" told her that her "mama never, ever come back."

As our trust grew, she told me more about her version of the day we met. She was told in the morning of that day that she would have a mama. She was very excited.

There was a picture from the orphanage of her standing in front of her class with a big smile on her face. She told me that she was telling all the children, "Today, I find my mama." She said, upon questioning, that this news was met with sadness from the others. "They sad. They no find their mamas."

The children were all put down for the afternoon nap. After all the children fell asleep, Jaclyn was awakened and taken from the room. She was given a "pur-dee dress" to wear for the first time ever. ("Hey, what happened to my China dress?" she asked as she recounted this. I showed her that it had been stored away as a treasured keepsake.) She was not permitted to say good-bye to any of her friends; they were all asleep. Jaclyn was still troubled by the fact that she was not able to say good-bye to her baby. I knew she imagined his grief when he awoke and found her gone.

She had never been in a car before and rode in one for the first time on her way to meet us at the Office of Civil Affairs. On the way there she vomited in her teacher's hand. "But I not get my dress messy!" she said with pride. Before they left, she was given the teddy bear I had sent her weeks earlier. She had never seen it before.

She was very, very disappointed when she saw me. So much for first impressions. I had asked her many times what she didn't like about me when she first saw me. Jaclyn, who now understood the concepts of tact and hurt feelings, was reluctant to level with me.

"Was it my blond hair that you didn't like?" I asked gently.

"No," she said before tentatively broaching this truth, "but your nose and eyes a little bit YUCKY!" We laughed together.

Her comment triggered my memory of her putting her eyes right up to mine on our second day as mother and daughter. She was fascinated with my mascaraed lashes, something she had clearly never seen before, and tentatively touched them while examining them closely. I knew that my eyes, which are green, could in no way compare in beauty to the almond eyes that were smiling back at me.

"I want China mama! But now I like this-a mama!" she said with a laugh, as if to say, "What could I have been thinking?"

I never thought the question marks of her past would have any answers. But Jaclyn held on to these memories with the same determined tenaciousness that she used to approach life. If only all the memories were not so sad. If only she had one happy memory of her past life to cling to. So far there had been none.

Her past became like a nameless, faceless ghost who now lived with us, too, just like the memory of Xiao Mei Mei. There was no escape; it was always there. Not only did Jaclyn have amazing recall of her past, but she also wanted to understand other children's pasts, too. Maybe this need was based on the principle of "misery loves company." Maybe it just gave her more information to use to sort out what her expectations should be in this life.

Jaclyn viewed the world, as we all do, through the lens of her experience. She had a fierce sense of justice and tried hard to reconcile her beliefs about what was fair with her life so far. Rick, an attorney, finally had hope that one of his six children would follow in his footsteps.

I was not sure if all the older children in the orphanage routinely shared their pasts in a "What's your story, kid?" mode or if they hid them in secret shame. But I did know that Jaclyn knew details of her best friend's frightening abandonment. What I didn't know was that she had also carefully reviewed the photo album of her little sister Christy's adoption from China, which included photos of the sidewalk where she had been abandoned when she was a few days old. Given Jaclyn's nature, I guess I should not have been entirely surprised by what came next.

The girls were snuggling together in my bed while I got ready for work one day when Jaclyn turned to her sister and said, "Christ-ta-tee, why your China mama leave you on the ground?" I gasped as I heard the question and watched the puzzled look form on Christy's face; she had no idea of what was being asked.

Jaclyn felt tremendous anger at her China mama in spite of my best efforts to help her understand why parents sometimes cannot care for their children. I did not want her to taint Christy's view of her birth mother, too, so I stepped in and said, "Jaclyn, we believe that Christy's China mama might have been very sick and could not take care of baby Christy. So she took her to a safe place where people would help take care of her until her new mama could come for her."

Jaclyn looked at me skeptically.

"Christ-ta-tee, where your daddy go? He die?" Jaclyn knew now that a mama was not the only one who had responsibility for a child. She wanted a full accounting of why Christy's daddy did not step up to the plate. Before I could interject, Christy, who had no idea what was being asked, said solemnly, "Yes!"

"Oh," Jaclyn said to me as she accepted this at face value. "Her daddy die." I began again my attempt to change her understanding of all this. I struggled to find the right words to explain to one so young the complicated economic, social, and political circumstances that control mothers' decisions in the country that I had come to love. Jaclyn listened patiently but then insisted that I hear her, too.

"Mama," she said, with emotion born of anger in her voice, "a baby on the *ground*! A baby can't walk. A baby can't talk. A baby no have even teeth. Cars come by! *A baby get hurt!* That DISGUSTING!" She set her little chin in defiance. She had meted out her judgment of this action. And, as always with Jaclyn, there was no dissuading her. She was a child who spoke her own truth.

All this before 7:30 A.M.; no wonder I was always late for work.

In spite of the warning I had received from other adoptive parents about the adoption themes in the movie *Stuart Little*, I took Kate and Jaclyn to see the movie. The kids wanted to go, and I figured that Jaclyn was too young to understand any confusing adoption messages. In fact, her favorite movie was *Annie*. I was concerned at first when this was the movie that she insisted on watching over and over. But if she saw any parallel between its story and her former life, she did not reveal it. She delighted in mimicking the dialogue and loved to tell me, after watching me dress for work, "You're never fully dressed without a smile!" And although you could make a compelling argument that her theme song should be "It's the Hard-Knock Life," the one she loved to sing was "Tomorrow." Somehow, its message of hope was fitting.

I didn't think twice about the impact of this movie as we chose our seats in the tiny neighborhood theater. When would I ever learn not to underestimate Jaclyn?

One of the first scenes in the movie showed the prospective adoptive parents going to an orphanage to select a child. Jaclyn watched it all wide-eyed, then turned to me in the darkened theater and asked a new question, "Mama, why you pick *me*?"

Unlike most of her questions, this one was easy to answer.

"Because I loved you so much," I said with a lump in my throat, even though I knew the real answer was that God had picked us for each other.

She thought about this for a moment, but then said sadly in almost a whisper, "Why you not pick Xiao Mei Mei?"

A true "Jaclyn question" was one for which there was no answer. How could I ever begin to explain how I had left any of them behind?

But the movie also gave her some new perspective. That night when she said her prayers, she used still another new word: *orphan*. She began, as she always did, with prayers for her baby: "Dear God, Bless Xiao Mei Mei, an ORPHAN," she said. "He so sad. He so scared. He have a birthday. He bigger now. Help him find a mama. He a good boy. He help his mama. Bless Jaclyn, an *orphan*. Bless Jin Xun Li, an *orphan*. Bless Xi Lan, an *orphan*. Bless Gua Hoo Lee, an *orphan*. Amen."

I lay there unsure of what I was to say next.

"Jaclyn," I began, "you're not an orphan. You have a family. So do Jin Xun Li and Xi Lan."

She looked into my eyes sadly. "Mama," she said with a faraway look on her face, "we all *orphans* together."

I knew her well enough to tell when her opinion was intractable; there was no room for persuading her this time. It was clear that in her eyes, even a new family wasn't enough to make you forget the reality of who you once were.

But the past had many unanswered questions for her, too. Jaclyn came downstairs early one morning as I was exercising and watched me doing my sit-ups. I tried to shoo her away, but she had questions and was not leaving without answers.

"Why you adopt Christ-ta-tee before Jaclyn?" she demanded to know. "She just a little baby. Why I have to wait until I a big girl to find a mama?" Jaclyn, like most small children, had a need for things to be fair and seem just. She knew that there was nothing fair about her and all her friends waiting while babies were adopted regularly at her orphanage. She demanded to understand that for which there was no explanation except the truth, and the truth that most people prefer to adopt infants was one that I didn't want her to know. So she picked at this issue like a scab that she couldn't let heal. She asked me over and over for the reason why she waited for what seemed to her an eternity to "find a mama."

I had never been able to explain to her satisfaction the complicated series of events that brought her to us. How could I explain to a small child that a paperwork snafu trapped her while at least two wonderful families tried desperately to adopt her? So once again I found myself trying to answer a "Jaclyn question."

"Why I wait so long?" she begged to know as she stood over me. "Why you not get me *first*?" For the umpteenth time, I tried to explain.

"Your papers were all messy," I said, attempting to use words appropriate for a four-year-old. I knew she understood that papers were part of the adoption process. After all, she had asked me repeatedly about the papers needed to bring Xiao Mei Mei home.

"Who messy my papers?" she demanded to know, hands on her hips, with a set look on her face. "What her name?"

Jaclyn wanted justice. She needed to know who was to blame for all she endured in her long wait.

"The government," I responded weakly as I thought of the faceless, overworked, understaffed bureaucracy that was responsible for international adoptions proceeding at a snail's pace while tiny souls languished.

"Hfff," snorted Jaclyn, "I HATE gubberment."

Me, too, kid. Me too.

Chapter Seventeen

Two Steps Forward . . . Three Steps Back

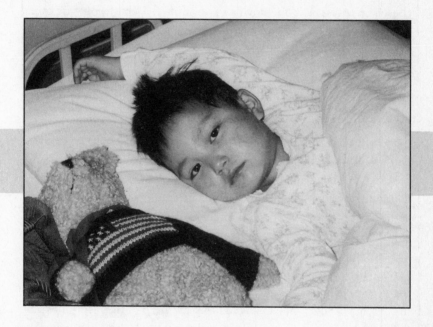

If you have faith as a grain of mustard seed . . . nothing shall be impossible unto you.
—Matthew 17:20

Once the decision was made that my sister Laura would pursue the adoption of Xiao Mei Mei, I thought that the pain and the roller coaster of uncertainty about what to do about this child would be over. We had a plan now. What I didn't realize was that the roller coaster would now be rolling ahead in earnest. The first few weeks proved to be filled with peaks of hope followed by downward slides of doubt and despair.

There were lots of obstacles ahead. We had to meet all the requirements of the U.S. Immigration and Naturalization Service in addition to those imposed by the Chinese government. Laura's newly adopted child, Willow, needed to be a citizen before a second adoption could be pursued. In Michigan, this was a long process. Laura did some research and found out that the head of the Senate Committee on Immigration and Naturalization was Spence Abraham, coincidently a Michigan senator. Laura, though one of the shyest people I know, sat down and wrote an amazing letter to him. In it she described the love that Jaclyn had for her baby and told of her endless prayers to God on his behalf. She told the story of Jaclyn's determination to bring her baby home and begged the senator for help. She explained that she needed the favor of expedited citizenship for her newly adopted daughter in order to pursue the adoption of Jaclyn's baby.

Meanwhile, working on the premise that only six degrees of separation lie between each of us, Jeff worked on finding a connection to this man. And he did. Someone knew someone who knew someone in his office, and the letter was hand-delivered. Three days later, Laura's phone rang.

"I'm an aide to Senator Spence Abraham," the caller said. "We've all read your letter and are in tears. Tell me what the senator can do to help bring Jaclyn's baby here, and he'll do it." So instead of the usual six-month wait, three weeks later Laura had not only the necessary citizenship papers in her hand but also the senator's promise to help speed immigration processing along once the Chinese officials had given their permission for the adoption.

But we had more immediate financial concerns. How would we pay for this adoption? Laura and Jeff had just come back from China in November. The costs seemed prohibitive. Rick and I vowed to help, but they knew we were whistling through our hats. We had done two adoptions ourselves in the last two years. We didn't have two nickels to rub together.

But in the world of adoption we had learned much about faith. In amazing ways the money comes, and this time was no exception. I had continued to write about Jaclyn's quest for her baby. These writings were now posted on web sites and had been distributed through various Internet adoption groups. Several articles had appeared in newsletters and adoption publications.

As a result, Jaclyn now had fans. A woman in Minnesota, whom I would not recognize if I saw her on the street, had been following this story through her daughter-in-law, an adoptive mom. She paid all the initial fees—every cent. Another special family, which I had assisted with adoption, thanked me by sending a sizeable check to help bring Xiao Mei Mei home. Other gifts toward this cause trickled in, too. This generosity presented a different kind of struggle for my sister.

"I can't take the money," Laura said. "You know Mom and Dad taught us to be proud and not to accept charity."

"I know how you feel, Laura, but the money isn't for you," I said. "This is no time for pride. These gifts are for him, and if anyone ever needed help, it is this little guy. Let's just say a prayer of gratitude for these real-life angels."

And we weren't the only ones praying. My writings, through the miracle of the Internet, had moved far beyond the realm of the adoption community. I soon learned something new about the power of prayer. It multiplies. It multiplies in an exponential way.

As I shared the stories of Jaclyn's prayers and her quest for her baby, the letters came: "My prayer circle in New York is praying for Xiao Mei Mei . . . ," they wrote. "Our church in Arkansas is praying for him. . . ."

And "My mother and I pray for Jaclyn and Xiao Mei Mei every day. . . ." Also, "My daughter and daughter-in-law ask me every day if there is any word about Jaclyn's baby. Give Jaclyn a big hug from our entire Indian reservation. Please know you are all in our prayers. . . ." And from across the ocean in faraway England, "I have prayed that God would not forsake him. . . ."

I knew then that we don't suffer in vain. And Jaclyn's baby had suffered; there was no disputing the fact. Jaclyn had endlessly recited tales of his hunger, his cold, his fear, his tears, his pain, and his victimization. His eyes told the rest. But I now had the hope that through knowing him, through hearing his story, other lives might be changed. I knew mine had been. And if his story made just one more person interested in adoption, saved one more child, his suffering would not be in vain.

Jaclyn, meanwhile, kept our feet to the fire. There was never a day when she didn't talk about her baby, miss him, pray for him. And hearing her gut-wrenching pleas never got any easier; my heart was tugged raw.

Jaclyn also kept an eye on our progress. She carefully eavesdropped on many of the hushed phone conversations between my sister and me. She heard our harsh words, too. And since she was after all only four, she questioned me relentlessly about what was going on. I tried to evade her inquiries, put her off, make only vague promises, but she knew. She always knew. Gradually I had introduced the idea of Xiao Mei Mei going to her aunt's house. She would set her chin when she heard this plan, but she never responded to it.

Because she did not know the difficulty of what she was asking for, how hard it was to get a child registered for adoption, how difficult identified adoptions were to do, she never doubted that it would happen. For her, it was always a matter of *when*. And her faith in me, her trust that her mama could do this one thing, made me forge ahead without being frozen by the fear that it was too difficult, by the fear that I would fail her. Even when doubt nagged at me, when common sense told me it would not happen, her utter trust that it would happen kept me from wavering.

But the winter of 1999 brought with it a storm of other trials. My work situation became mired in the ugliness of small-town, small-minded politics. Divorce and cancer engulfed some of those we loved. The endless problems of each day left me sleepless at night. I was barely able to function. I lost my way amid the swirling myriad of problems engulfing me.

The result was that my progress in assisting with Xiao Mei Mei's adoption was slowed. But Jaclyn had not stopped her petitions to God on his behalf.

I still wasn't sure then how much Jaclyn could possibly understand about the concept of prayer, but I knew she believed that God would help her find Xiao Mei Mei a mama, and that God would help him not to be afraid. In return, she promised God that "he a good boy." And, after a time, she made me believe. I knew how her pleas ripped a hole in her father Rick's heart; I could only imagine how her innocent words, her trusting faith, affected her Heavenly Father.

Still afraid of her disappointment if all our efforts failed, I continued to try to hide from Jaclyn all that was transpiring to bring him here. How naive that was of me; there was no hiding anything from Jaclyn. She was hypervigilant in the way that abused children are and had a tenaciousness that would put even the best *National Enquirer* reporter to shame. She continued to eavesdrop and question everything relentlessly. She would go through drawers and garbage cans looking for clues and questioning the contents. As much as I tried, there was no putting her off with a vague response. There was simply no escaping her relentless pleas.

Finally, one March night, after she told God again how cold Xiao Mei Mei was, she confronted me.

"Mama," she said, "I talk-ee you." She patted the spot on the bed next to her, and I lay down. She gently took my face between her hands and held my gaze with her own sad eyes. "When Xiao Mei Mei get here?" I mumbled a response, trying to evade her once again.

"Mama," she said, "I *need* him. I NEED him." I inhaled slowly. This was a word she had never used before, and the fact that she used it so appropriately was startling. And then she made an amazing revelation about her understanding of the adoption process: "I no see you do the paper, Mama. I can't do it. It too hard for me. I need you do the paper."

I was found wanting; I had not been working on the process the way I should be. How in the world did she know? There was no escaping her searing gaze.

She continued, "Tomorrow, Mama. You work fast. Then you come home and you do the paper, OK?" I nodded mutely, anxious to leave her bed before I began to cry.

Her words haunted me as I tried to escape into sleep. The refrain "Mama, I NEED him" played over and over in my mind. And what if he didn't make his way here? "Oh, God," I prayed silently, "please help."

The dossier was filed with baited breath. Then the hard part started: the wait. Every day Jaclyn's prayers continued. Every day she asked me how long it would be until we could get her baby. Every day I tried to avoid her searching eyes.

Chapter Eighteen

The Darkest Hour

A friend is someone who knows the song in your heart and can sing it back to you
when you have forgotten the words.
—Unknown

As the heartaches piled up, I began to believe I would fall into the darkness of depression, a destination that filled me with fear. I had days when I felt I was hanging on to the edge of that dark pit by my fingertips and if I dared to reach my arms up for help, I would lose my grip and fall in.

Concurrent with this, or most probably because of it, Jaclyn, who could sense a person's weakness, began what could only be described as a reign of terror. She would only drink from the red cup. She would only eat with the tiny white fork. She demanded pickles and peanuts for breakfast and would stubbornly refuse to eat anything else. She pitched fits because I would not let her bring Popsicles to school in her lunch box. She would not wear what I laid out for school, and I was afraid the Department of Social Services would ring my doorbell if I let her wear what she selected. Everything now was a battle. She would not share. She took things from her sisters. She fought with them constantly. She woke up crabby and whining. She went to bed crabby and whining. She was crabby and whining every moment in between. She had meltdowns that could be heard in the next county; I shut all the windows as she screamed so that the neighbors would not report us as suspected child abusers.

On a good day, Jaclyn was an exhausting child to parent. This was a child who would not let me rest. She was a dizzying whirlwind of energy. Her relentless questions, her challenging of the rules at every turn, her secret manipulations, kept me always in a state of alert. Her protracted negotiations and the explosive eruptions in her struggle for power and control exhausted me. Trying to stay ahead of her was hopeless. Trying to stay even wasn't even plausible. On my best day, I was two steps behind. At least. And some days I could hardly put one foot in front of the other.

But on a bad day . . . on a bad day I was sure that the fates had played a nasty trick on me by making me her mother. In the battle of the wills, my own strong will was no match for hers. Not even close.

"Do you realize what a milestone you've reached?" Carl, an adoptive father, told me. "Now she feels safe enough to show you her worst behavior and trusts that you will still love her. Congratulations!"

But it was hard to see the victory in this. And in spite of my husband's repeated assurances that it certainly would get easier, I began to question God's wisdom in giving this child to me.

My mother, a very wise woman, always said that when you really needed it, God had a way of sending you a hug. On one of my darkest days, I got a wonderful note from a family across the ocean, one that I had never met. They had been following my writings about Jaclyn and her baby. In the note, they shared how knowing Jaclyn's story had touched their lives and how desperately they prayed for Xiao Mei Mei's adoption. The letter said, in part: "My husband is a kind and compassionate man who can't bear the thought of children suffering and he thinks that your daughter is an exceptionally brave and resilient little girl. The Daddy in him wants to make her feel better, to let her know that even all this distance away there are people who care about her. I would like to add that I think about you and the challenges that parenting such a hurt child must bring. You are obviously the mother Jaclyn desperately needs to help her come to terms with her painful past. Special children like these are given to the parents who can cope, and I find that a great inspiration and strive to live up to the trust that God has put in us as parents."

What an *enormous* hug. It was just what I needed to center myself. The same characteristics that could bring me to my knees were, of course, the ones that this child needed to help her survive all the pain and loss. She was, after all, the one to whom the other children had brought their grievance about missing a meal when we visited the orphanage. She was the one who boldly confronted the teacher about this issue, demanding an explanation on behalf of her friends. She was the one who would not be quieted. She was the one who stood up to the "bad big boys" who were a full head taller than she was to protect her baby. My Jaclyn. The bravest soul I knew.

But there was more. This wonderful family of strangers yet friends in the world of adoption asked if they could send Jaclyn a gift. I wrote back suggesting that if they would like to do so, I would suggest that they help another child in her name.

And so they did. In Jaclyn's name, they sponsored a child in China with Down's syndrome. They sent us his picture and some information about him with this note: "I hope that one day it will comfort Jaclyn to know that her story touched others and led to children being helped."

There were many Down's syndrome children and disabled children at Jaclyn's orphanage; she had spoken about them several times. She told me that they were segregated from the other kids and she was told not to associate with them because they were the "messy, ugly" kids. But luckily my Jaclyn made her own judgments and seemed to have ignored this directive; she has a heart full of compassion. I knew that this kindness, in her name, would touch her deeply one day.

And there was more. A package arrived from overseas addressed to Jaclyn. And inside was an incredible gift. The same family had commissioned a local artist to make a stained glass sun catcher depicting a black-haired angel holding "her baby" in its arms. It is meant, of course, to symbolize Jaclyn and Xiao Mei Mei. And it was without a doubt the most perfect gift ever. Jaclyn was absolutely thrilled with it and proudly admired it as it was hung in our front window.

Enclosed was a note from her new friends: "I am sure that Jaclyn's heartrending prayers for her baby must be being heard, and that one day they will be reunited. How could even the Almighty fail to be moved by such passionate and persistent pleas for Xiao Mei Mei?"

What a hug! It lifted me up so high that I could see what mattered again.

But I was not the only one who was filled with fear. Jaclyn's fear crept up on her without warning and ultimately spilled over onto all of us. Of course, Jaclyn had been terrified at our first meeting; her animal-like howls were ample evidence. But as bravely as she had faced all that her new life brought with it, fear was always simmering below the surface.

The fears were different now. She trusted us to give her food; her secret stashes had disappeared. She trusted us not to hurt her; her increasingly bold misbehavior was the result. She trusted us not to shut her bedroom door; her fear of the dark was a little less frantic. But her most overwhelming fear, that of keeping her place in our lives, was still present. Sometimes we would go weeks without any evidence of it, but then it would boil over in ways that pained me.

We eagerly anticipated the visit in April of my hero and now dear friend, Snow Wu, executive director of the Great Wall China Adoption agency. As Jaclyn listened to our excited talk, she also was excited that "Snow White" was coming to visit. We gently explained that it was not a Disney character that we were expecting but a very special woman who had helped to make her our daughter and who helped other children in China find homes.

"How she do it?" Jaclyn queried. "She ask the baby you want this-a family or this-a one?" She was confused, since she knew she'd had no choice in this matter and, if truth be told, would not have chosen the mother with the yucky eyes and nose if a Chinese mom had been available. I tried to break down the process into words she could comprehend.

"Snow White help Xiao Mei Mei find a mama? She bring my baby here?" she asked as she began to grasp the power of this woman. But along with her excitement at meeting a person who could help with her quest came fear. It bubbled up and spilled over before I ever saw it coming.

"Mama, tell Snow White I don't want to go to some other family. I don't want to go to 'nother house. I want to stay here!" Where this sudden outburst came from, I couldn't know. But it was clear that she was terrified of the presence of a woman with such power over lives. After all, if she was the one who found families for kids, how did Jaclyn know that she could not undo this process, too?

I was taken by surprise by this demon; we had gone so long now without seeing him. So I went over again how Jaclyn was part of our family for always and would not go away. When she met Snow, all her brave intent to advocate for her baby quickly faded. Her upbringing came to the surface; she was respectful of all Chinese adults and intimidated in their presence. But a few nights later, the demon was back.

"Mama," she said at bedtime, "I want to stay here FOREVER. Can I stay here *forever?*" And again I went through the cycle of assurances.

The next day, Rick and I both awoke early and went down to the basement to work on a project. Suddenly I heard a frantic wail and the harsh, gasping sobs that only Jaclyn could make when she was overcome by grief. I rushed upstairs. She was curled up in the fetal position in our empty bed, racked with sobs. When I finally calmed her enough so that she could speak, her words spewed forth in an accusatory manner. "Where you go?"

When Jaclyn had first come home, she had a predictable early morning ritual. Even when her eyes were still swollen from sleep, she would run as fast as she could down the stairs to find me. So frantic was her need to know I was still there that it eradicated her fear of moving through a still dark house. Jaclyn had proved not to be a morning person, so this routine had changed dramatically as her security in our presence deepened. Now she sleepily sought us out, walking slowly, and seemed to need only a few snuggly hugs to ease her into wakefulness.

But when I was not in the predictable place, all the terror erupted inside her again.

Oh, dear child, I wondered as I soothed her gently, how long will it be until you know that I will not go?

As the dark days of waiting for news marched ever forward, I found my own fears often giving way to despair. And even Jaclyn momentarily lost heart. Even she faltered.

As each bedtime approached, my heart began to fill with trepidation. I sometimes silently hoped that she would not want to talk, that she would simply make her endless pleas to God for her baby's safety and then let me escape without more. Because the truth was, I could not take any more. The pain and sadness that came with the knowledge of where she had been and what she was thinking flooded my heart so that it often felt as if I couldn't hold it all in for her sake any longer. And just when I would bob up long enough to grasp another breath, she would get me again.

Only this time, the target of her anger was not Chinese mothers and government and endless paperwork systems. This time she aimed higher.

Our conversation started out innocuously, as many of them did.

"Mama," Jaclyn said with authority, "everybody have a job!"

"Yes, Jaclyn, that's right," I responded.

"Your job ME!" she said with finality. I smiled to myself as I thought that she had no idea how true that was. So then, thinking she would respond that going to school was her job, I asked her what she thought her job was.

"My job Xiao Mei Mei," she said without even stopping to think. I looked at her silently.

She was now ready to pray: "Dear God, Xiao Mei Mei scared. He a little boy. He my baby. YOU don't take good care of him in BAD China. I take care of him. We pay the money; bring him to me. Amen."

I was silent contemplating this new source of blame. And I was deeply pained once again at her reflection on her homeland. I could think of nothing to say, so I just looked into her eyes silently.

And then she added this whispered request, "Don't get lost, Mama. Don't ever get lost from me."

I reassured her, then headed downstairs and sobbed. For her, for Xiao Mei Mei, for all those that she believed that God had forsaken.

Chapter Nineteen

The Four Freedoms

It is not for him to pride himself who loveth his own country, but rather for him
who loveth the whole world. The earth is but one country and mankind its citizens.
—Bahá Alláh

Jaclyn's school had an end-of-the-year program. The backyard of the school was brightly decorated with banners and balloons. A makeshift stage was assembled on the grass. Parents sat on lawn chairs, wearing sweatshirts to ward off the morning chill. Dads were laden down with videotape recorders and cameras. Kate, Christy, and I sat together on a blanket on the lawn waiting for the program to begin.

The teacher walked on stage and announced brightly, "Since our holiday program celebrated diversity, we thought that we would have a program to celebrate the *one* thing that we all have in common—we are *all* Americans!"

I swallowed hard. Jaclyn was a citizen of the People's Republic of China; she had not yet been granted citizenship. Then the children trooped out. To my amazement I watched Jaclyn, hand somberly over her heart, recite the Pledge of Allegiance with all the other children. I watched her sing "My Country 'Tis of Thee." I watched her recite all fifty states; my favorite was the one she called "New Hampster."

And then it was her turn for the spotlight. They brought her forward in a quartet to sing "It's a Grand Old Flag." They had her decked out in a wreath of red, white, and blue stars. She was wearing an American flag vest and matching shirt. She marched and saluted sharply. And in her hand she proudly waved an American flag.

I felt a pang of conscience. Somehow it all seemed a little too much like brainwashing. She had not even been in this country a year. Could she even remember the flag of her homeland? And there was no denying that she had been taken against her will. I could still see her planted feet, can still hear her screams, as she was forcibly loaded into our car. She had told me repeatedly about her crushing disappointment that her parents were foreigners. At some level she understood that this meant she had to leave her homeland.

I remembered her initial silence in this country, made more pronounced by its stark contrast to her usual animated chatter, as she found herself immersed in a strange land where no one spoke her language. And most of all I remembered her confused misgivings when it was time to leave China on our last trip there. I remembered her telling me how she wanted to stay in China. How could I ever forget her saying, "I no like everybody look like Mama, nobody look like Jaclyn. In China, I understand what everybody saying."

But all these things were rationalized away by saying that we adults knew what was best for her. It was best for her to have a family, even one in a foreign land. It was best for her to be a citizen of the United States; to grow up to know freedoms that can barely be imagined in her homeland. I felt then that U.S. citizenship was one of the great gifts I could bestow on her. Why then did I feel such a pang of guilt watching her decked out as a Yankee Doodle Dandy?

And then I remembered another reality. The mob I saw, on three different trips to China, in front of the U.S. embassy. It was a line that did not move, that pressed against the embassy gates that I so easily walked through. It was a crowd of faces filled with looks of resignation and infinite patience. They waited for days on end for the rarely meted out approvals that would result in the privilege of a visit to the United States. And I remembered all those who said, with truth in their eyes, "lucky baby" when they found out she was coming to America. Some of that sentiment may have been just about the fact that she now had a family. Some might have been about their visions of untold riches in the land of Mickey Mouse. But a few might have dared to envy the freedom that they knew was awaiting her here.

So, the child who came home on the July Fourth weekend a year ago had now become a Yankee Doodle Dandy. She could no longer speak her native language and spoke only disparagingly of her homeland. She had finally convinced me to let her drop out of Chinese school. She now turned her head when Chinese was spoken to her. She often told her Chinese sister about all the things she now loved that they did not have in China. I kept hoping that this would change as I reinforced all that there was to love in China and shared with her my appreciation for its beauty, its culture, and its rich history. But knowing full well how stubborn she could be, I did not have much hope that I would change her mind any time soon.

I still believed that we did the right thing in bringing her here. But I also knew we did it at a steep price—to forever change who she was.

No wonder that, once again, I was the only mom watching the program with tears in her eyes.

Finally, in July, the long-awaited letter arrived scheduling Jaclyn's citizenship interview. I was so excited I couldn't wait to share the news with her.

"Jaclyn, guess what?" I began. "You're going to be an American citizen!" She gave me a puzzled look, so I went on, "Mommy and Daddy are going to take you to a government office—"

"NO!" she howled in fear and rage, "I WANT TO STAY HERE!" I could have kicked myself. This was the kid who had already told me she hates "gubberment." How could I not have known that this would terrify her? So after reassuring her that of course she was here to stay, I tried again.

"This meeting means you are going to be an American just like Mommy and Daddy and Katie and Christy."

"Oh," she said evenly. "I no be Chinese anymore? When I grow up I not be Chinese lady? I be lady that look like Mama?" Hmmm . . . I was stuck now. I tried to tell her that she would always be Chinese but that now she would stay in America.

"This house America?" she asked. I weakly nodded and decide to drop it for the time being.

However, Jaclyn did not forget, and the next day she approached me with this: "Mama, next week when I go to grand old flag—"

I interrupted her by saying, "How do you know there will be a grand old flag?"

"I look in Christ-ta-tee's picture book," she told me. "You say Christ-ta-tee already go there."

She was amazingly resourceful. She apparently had decided to figure this out on her own. Although the concept was too nebulous for her to comprehend, she did understand that this was something special.

She was very excited about helping me with her citizenship announcements. She busied herself putting on the return address labels upside down, folding the announcements so they couldn't fit into the envelopes but trying to stuff them in anyway, and vigorously overlicking the stamps. Christy tried to get in on the action but was promptly shooed away.

"Christ-ta-tee," Jaclyn said sternly, "you break all our hard work. I help Mama. This not for babies!" We continued to work together in silence on the pile of announcements.

"Mama," Jaclyn said wistfully, "can I send one to Jin Xun Li? I want her know." Jaclyn was heartbroken that she and her friend had not been able to keep in closer touch. I promised Jaclyn we could send her one.

"What about Xiao Mei Mei?" she added softly. "Please, please I send one to Xiao Mei Mei?" This request I had to refuse, trying to explain that he could not get mail at the orphanage. But I told her we could put one away for him, and she carefully picked one out and brought me an envelope.

"Please, Mama, put Xiao Mei Mei's name on it so I can see it. I save it for him," she said.

He was always with us. He was always in her heart. Everything that was special in her life lost some of its bang if it couldn't be shared with her beloved baby.

I know he would be proud of you, Jaclyn, on your special day, I said to myself. I sure am.

The day began in typical Jaclyn fashion. She woke the household at 6:30 A.M. with exuberant cries of "Wake up! It my grand old flag day!" It was not long, however, before she was in a snit. She protested angrily at my request that she wash herself in the shower. The child who a year ago in China washed herself like a surgeon, then cleaned the tub afterward, could somehow no longer do so. In fact, she didn't feel like cooperating at all. This was the way Jaclyn dealt with her anxiety, or more correctly didn't deal with it. When she was not sure what would happen next, she spun out of control. So on this auspicious day, Jaclyn began with a stint in the time-out chair until she could calm herself.

We reached the immigration office, and an apprehensive Jaclyn insisted on sitting on my lap. Finally, it was our turn to meet with the immigration officer. He ushered us into his office and designated a chair for Jaclyn to sit in. "I no like green! I not sit in the green chair!" she said emphatically while planting herself in a blue chair.

Her father, trying to cooperate with the man who had the authority with one fell swoop of his pen to grant the citizenship prize to her, gently tried to coax her into the chair he had indicated. She was not budging. She was, after all, going to be an American. Americans don't unquestioningly obey authority figures. Americans have their own ideas.

To my surprise, the officer, like most adults who met Jaclyn, seemed anxious to please her. "We have red chairs, too," he said, indicating one at the end of the row. "Would you rather sit in the red chair?" Jaclyn gave the red chair a dismissive glance. She had chosen her seat.

She was not seated long. We all smiled as we turned in her old green card; she hardly resembled the sad child with the badly cropped hair in the picture.

"I like your hair much better now," the officer said with a smile. Jaclyn smiled back. She then began to examine the contents of his desk.

"What that, Mama?" she said, pointing to one item. "It's glue," I answered. Jaclyn was very impressed by this. At her school, only the most responsible children were allowed to handle glue by themselves. Clearly the man had gone up a notch in her estimation since he was entrusted with his own glue.

The officer asked us several routine questions. He then closed the file, thinking that, since his questions were answered, the interview had concluded. But Jaclyn now had her questions.

"Can I see these?" she asked the man, indicating the collection of family photos on his desk.

"Who that?" she asked as he showed her each picture in turn. We then learned way more than we needed to know about the immigration officer, his stepchildren, and his various assorted family relationships.

"Where you little kids?" Jaclyn asked, with obvious disappointment that none of the photos had children in them. "You got any little kids?" The officer shook his head no. Jaclyn was not sure about the veracity of this response. She went to the bulletin board across from his desk and pointed to all the photos of him with other children, like her, that he had helped make citizens.

"Who those kids?" she asked. "They you kids?"

"No," he said solemnly. "But sometimes they're just so cute I wish they were," he quietly added while smiling at her.

We took our photos to mark the occasion, and Jaclyn happily thanked the man as she left. Her relief was almost palpable. She was leaving with the same adults she came with; this was a good thing.

We took her out to brunch to celebrate. As always, Xiao Mei Mei was on her mind. "Can I go, too, when Xiao Mei Mei go to grand old flag?" she asked. "I have to tell him what to do." She was a veteran of the system now. I told her I was sure that Aunt Laura would allow this.

Rick and I talked about how far she had come from "the little girl in the green coat" whose picture we had loved for so long. For the first time, Jaclyn talked about the infamous green coat.

"I tell the teacher I cold so she get it for me. But I not get to wear it every day. Some days the other kids wear it." She owned nothing.

She told the waitress how she wanted her eggs. "I not want them like this," she said making a stirring motion. "I want the kind with little circle that yellow and other little circle around it." She used her fingers to indicate the circles and made all the adults understand perfectly that Miss Jaclyn wanted her eggs sunny side up. Although I was still unsure what, if anything, about this day she understood, something made her reflect about her old life much more than she usually did.

"In China, I only get a little egg, not very much, for a treat," she said matter-of-factly. "I eat rice for breakfast. We no have lunch. I eat rice for dinner." And then, after pondering this, she added, "The kids take Xiao Mei Mei's food. I share with him."

Freedom from want, dear child. This day means freedom from want.

As Rick helped buckle her into her car seat, I watched his face carefully. On this joyful day, it was lined with sadness. I didn't have to ask the reason why. I knew firsthand what a toll it took on your soul to hear Jaclyn talk about her past. Before today, I had been the sole repository of her pain. Now we could share this pain, too.

On the long ride home, she continued to reflect upon her former life. She rarely talked about her past without the cover of darkness. But from the safety of her car seat, with no one's eyes to look into, she told us, "In China, teacher get mad at me all the time for talking. I want to talk to my baby. I want to talk to the kids. The other kids want to talk, too."

Is the most basic tenet of freedom of speech the right to actually speak at all? Then the freedom to speak and the freedom of speech have been granted to you, Jaclyn. In this country, we allow children to be heard, too.

"They hit me when I talk," she said. "I no say 'I sorry,' because they hurt me very bad. It make red on me. They hit me with the black thing. Like a belt but you don't wear it." We were silent.

"They hit the other kids, too. But they hit me because I talk the most. They no have time-out chair in China. Time-out chair is this one," she said as she held her arms straight out at her sides. "They make me do this, and it hurt very bad."

We assured her that she would never be hurt again. Freedom from fear, dear child. This day means freedom from fear.

We drove in silence. It was a gorgeous, sunny day and the clouds were full and fluffy in the sky. Jaclyn pointed to an unusually beautiful formation of them and asked, "Mama, is that where the angels sleep?" I looked to where she was pointing.

"I don't know," I said. "What do you think?"

"I think so," Jaclyn said. She pondered this and then asked, "Mama, when we go to Heaven and be angels, what we do all day?"

"I'm not sure, Jaclyn," I said. "Maybe we do kind things for other people?" She was clearly disappointed by this answer.

"What about toys?" she asked. "They got any toys in Heaven?"

I told her yes, sure that any other answer would make Heaven seem like a less than desirable place to end up.

"How the toys get to Heaven?" she asked. "Do toys die, too?" I shrugged, helpless to find an answer to this.

Freedom of religion, dear child. The freedom to worship and believe all that your faith tells you is true. This, too, has been accorded you.

Jaclyn then told me, "I not go live in China again." I indicated that she was right, she lived in America now. She then thought about this more.

"I not sleep in China anymore."

Within minutes, lulled by the motion of the car and her spent emotions, she was asleep.

Sleep well, dear child. You can now rest. You are home.

Chapter Twenty

The Long-Awaited News

Where there is great love there are always miracles.
—Willa Cather

In July of 2000, *months after the dossier* had been filed, we had some preliminary news from Snow. She had been working fiendishly and the result was that a "promise" had been made that Laura and Jeff could adopt Xiao Mei Mei. It was a verbal promise, but from a person in the Chinese government with the authority to do so. Still I had to speak to Julie, the coordinator of the Great Wall staff in China, myself before I dared to believe it. Laura refused to believe the news until it was real, but we had begun to feel hopeful.

I determined not to tell Jaclyn of this promise. She was, after all, a child. But I could not keep it from her. I knew she was, if possible, more anxious for any word, any sign, than I was.

Rick and I decided to take the family out to dinner to celebrate this promise and to cautiously tell her the news. It was an unmitigated disaster. The wait at the restaurant was interminable, the kids hungry and cranky.

"Jaclyn, we have some news," I said. "A promise has been made by a very important official in China that Xiao Mei Mei can go and live with Aunt Laura and Uncle Jeff. It is only a promise, it isn't for sure yet. But we are very hopeful now that he will be able to come home soon."

She was quiet, so I went on. "If he really becomes Aunt Laura's son, he can spend the night at our house, and he will be very close by."

To our surprise, the news was not met with joy. Jaclyn set her chin stoically and bowed her head. Her crabbiness increased, and finally, as she began to spin out of control, I had to take her outside. After an hour's wait, we all left the restaurant still hungry and headed for McDonald's. It was a bust.

I figured that at bedtime I would finally hear what was up, and I did. Jaclyn was bitterly disappointed, even after all we had told her, that he was not to live in "this-a house" with her.

"Can he spend one night or lots of nights?" she asked.

"He can spend lots of nights," I said in a reassuring tone.

"Can he sleep right here?" she said, gesturing to a little space she had made in her bed for him. "Can he sleep in my bed with me?" I reassured her that he could. "Mama," she said solemnly, saving the most important question for last, "Can we take him to McDonald's?"

"Of course we will. We'll take him there all the time."

She was satisfied.

And then the angst was finally over. On August 2, 2000, while I was lunching with my boss and friend, Mary, my cell phone rang and, for once, I actually had it on. It was the official call from Great Wall adoption agency. The paperwork was in hand: Jaclyn's baby had been officially referred to my sister's family. He would be Jaclyn's cousin in America and would live twenty minutes away. He would have two families who would love him to pieces.

Mary looked at me, startled, as I burst into tears.

"What's wrong? What happened?" she said in alarm.

It took me several minutes to steady myself enough to say the words. "I guess God's finally gotten tired of Jaclyn's ceaseless prayers. Laura and Jeff got the referral. Jaclyn's baby is coming home!" I felt like screaming it from the rooftops.

Mary clapped her hands in delight. She had heard so much about this child that she had become caught up in the struggle herself.

"I've got to call Laura," I said as I punched the numbers with trembling hands. Laura and I cried together on the phone, thanking God over and over.

"You're coming to China with me, aren't you?" Laura said, even though she knew the answer.

"I hope they don't have to carry me out on a stretcher from all the emotion," I replied with a chuckle.

I called Rick and he shrieked with delight. "Don't worry, Cindy, I'll stay home with Kate and Christy so you can go," he said magnanimously. "I'd love to go myself, but I know how much it means to you. I can hardly wait to tell Jaclyn! I can just see her marching into that orphanage to claim him!" I hung up still in tears.

Lunch was forgotten. "Mary, come with us," I said imploringly. "I want you to see China. You'll love it. I want you to be there with me."

Mary, caught up in the excitement, agreed on the spot. This reunion, so long in coming, would be something to cherish.

Jaclyn had worked as hard as any other adoptive mom to bring her child home. I realized then that age didn't matter at all in making one's hopes a reality. All that mattered was that you had a dream that you clung to with your whole heart and soul, and that you were willing to do anything, sacrifice anything, cry and shout and beg and plead to make yourself heard if you had to, to make it a reality.

Now it was time to send in the balloons.

Now that it was official and the long-awaited referral was finally in hand, we couldn't wait to celebrate with Jaclyn. We decide to surprise her with the news by going out for a special dinner. This time we asked Jaclyn where she would like to eat, and, much to my husband's disappointment, we started out at McDonald's.

We told her the news at the restaurant and she jumped from her chair, ready to head to the airport, squealing, "Today? We go today?"

"No, Jaclyn, it will be a couple of weeks before you can go," Rick said.

"A couple mean two," she said, narrowing her eyes suspiciously. "How many?" she demanded to know. We told her we were not sure.

She no longer wanted to be Xiao Mei Mei's mom, as she was enjoying being a kid so much herself, but she still apparently wasn't sure that the adults in her life were up to the task.

"Daddy," she began solemnly, "you have to brush her hair like a boy." Jaclyn had trouble with personal pronouns, but we understood her, and Rick assured her that he was up to the task.

"Mama," she said authoritatively, "you have to get him little clothes like this." She pointed to her father's suit.

"Her a boy," she reminded us. "Her be a daddy when he grow up!"

Satisfied that we now understood what she expected, she chattered on for a while about the upcoming trip to China, and then decided to celebrate in Jaclyn fashion. This included spending time thoroughly examining her tongue and practicing sticking it out in front of the mirrored tiles on the wall. She made a nasty concoction in the lid of her sandwich box using barbecue sauce and pepper. She spilled her french fries on the floor, then mashed them into the tile with her sandals. She watched in riveted fascination, getting out of her seat for closer inspection, as a McDonald's worker emptied the trash can. She spun on the counter stools. She figured out a neat way to eat her ice cream cone by using her french fry as a little spoon.

Seeking reassurance again, she asked, "Will Xiao Mei Mei come to McDonald's with us?"

"Yes, Jaclyn. It will be one of the first places we take him in China," I told her.

And then, after careful reflection, she shared this with me: "Mama, Xiao Mei Mei can lick the ice cream cone. Then I can lick it. We can lick the same one! You know why?" I was puzzled by this thought and shook my head no.

"Because we FAMILY!" she said with a triumphant smile.

Yes, finally we would all be a family. Tears filled my eyes.

When we got home she begged to call Jin Xun Li to share her good news. This child, who had lived with them both, was perhaps the only one who could really understand what this triumph meant to her. She was delighted with the conversation and the excitement of her old friend.

When it was time for bed and she thought I was not watching, she went over to the picture of her baby that she kept in her room and kissed it gently.

"I see you soon, baby," she whispered softly to his photo.

And, because it was finally true, they were the sweetest words I had ever heard.

The joyous phone calls were followed a few days later by the FedEx delivery of his official paperwork. Laura rushed over to share it with me. The packet contained the documentation of his physical. He weighed twenty-two pounds and was thirty-three inches tall. He was three and a half years old. This, in and of itself, was enough to rip our hearts out.

But the picture . . . oh, the picture. His little face was black and blue, including two real shiners. I tried to hide the picture from Jaclyn, unable to bear her pain if she saw it. (Later, she found it anyway.) When she had seen the last photo of him, which had been sent by another adoptive family that had visited the orphanage, her face had frozen in pain. In that one, his nose appeared broken. There was no way to spin this, either. Jaclyn didn't believe for a moment any story about his getting hurt playing. She had told me several times about how, because of his small size and his meek manner, he was a target for bullying. She spoke about protecting him from the "bad big boys" and, given how bold she was and how strong, I was sure he was safe when he was in her care. No wonder she asked God every night, "Don't let him be afraid."

I'd heard it said that there is a correlation between how much children are loved and how beautiful they are. I knew this was true when I looked at Jaclyn's picture now and contrasted it with pictures of her a year ago in the institution. Then she had looked forlorn and pitiful. Now she radiated joy and good health. I saw this truth reflected in my niece's face, which grew ever more beautiful each day. So, given this theory, I figured that the next pictures of Jaclyn's baby should show a downright dapper young man.

But the real prize in the packet was information that gave me insight into how we live our lives with such limited understanding of the bigger plan. The official referral documents indicated that Tan Dong Jin was registered for adoption on the same day as my niece, Willow.

We verified that this meant he was one of the five "extra" children allowed to be registered for adoption because of the mix-up of the referral of Jin Xun Li. Had Laura and Jeff not lost the referral of Jin Xun Li, both Willow and Tan Dong Jin would most likely not have been registered for adoption. They not only would not have come to our family but also probably would never have been adopted by any family.

I thought of all the bitter tears we had all cried over the loss of the adoption referral of Jin Xun Li. Our plan had been that she would be the cousin of her best friend, Jaclyn, in America. Our plan seemed so perfect; how could her new family offer her more? But Jin Xun Li held, in her tiny hand, the red thread that linked us to the children that were meant to be ours. How God must have smiled when we finally understood the plan.

The next day, Jaclyn asked me, "What we do next tomorrow? And next tomorrow? How many next tomorrows until I get my baby?" I saw her rubbing his picture on her cheek and telling him that she missed him so much

Oh, God, I silently pleaded, just keep him safe until we get there.

Jaclyn's impatience grew daily.

She had prayed for him, oftentimes more than once, every night since she understood the concept of prayer. Although the themes and the requests on his behalf had varied, when she was tired she had one common prayer: "Dear God," she said, "Help Xiao Mei Mei find a mama. He scared; don't let him be afraid. He a good boy. Amen." I had heard this plea so often that I, too, could say it by heart without even having to think.

As the days passed waiting for the official permission from the Chinese government about when we would be allowed to travel, I continued to brace myself for the now familiar litany of prayer. But Jaclyn once again surprised me. From her changed tone, it was clear that she now truly believed that her baby would come home.

"Dear God," she began, "Xiao Mei Mei come to Aunt Lola's house. But he come here all the time. He can sleep with me. He can have fun. He can play toys. He can ride a bike."

At this juncture, she peeked through her eyelids and told me in a stage whisper, "Mama, we need get him a bike helmet." I nodded in assent as she continued her listing of all the wonderful things that would now be allowed him. "He can eat lunch." Jaclyn had told me over and over about the hunger that had walked with her. "He can eat dinner. He can have a snack! He can have a drink! He can brush his teeth! He can change clothes! He can take a bath or shower every day."

Again she peeked at me and stage-whispered, "I think he take a bath. He too scared of shower." I nodded again. She continued her talk with God: "He can have a towel! He not get cold anymore dry in air like in

China. I can wash his hair. I be very careful put water in back of his head so soap not hurt his eyes. Amen."

His new life: what a plethora of good fortune. I was humbled again by all the small things I took for granted that would be unimagined luxuries to this child as they were to Jaclyn. To have the bathtub to herself was undreamed of to her when she first joined our family.

The next day, new pictures arrived of him from the orphanage, and Laura hurried over to share them. This time his face looked perfect. In fact, he looked almost ethereal. It made me think of our first meeting and how horrified I was by his appearance. Sparse, thin hair barely covered his head. He was covered with sores and bug bites. Sticklike legs poked out from his pant legs. His face had the gaunt, emaciated, sickly pallor of the children who peered back silently from photographs of Auschwitz. Those are the faces that remind us of the price children pay when they live in a world without the love and protection of family.

I remembered thinking guiltily how lucky I felt that my adoption referral was for the healthy, stout child standing beside him. Would I have recoiled if I had received a referral like him?

But a funny thing happened along the way. As Jaclyn talked of him, as she shared stories about him, as she touted his virtues and talked of his sweetness, of his goodness, I began to love him, too. And that love changed everything. When I saw him now, I knew that he was the most beautiful child I had ever seen. I could only imagine how lucky I would have been had he been mine.

From the photo he stared back at us seriously, and both Laura and I marveled at how much taller he seemed. But so thin, so unbelievably emaciated. I told Jaclyn we had new pictures and that he looked happy in the pictures. After the ones sent by the other adoptive family, where he was visibly black and blue (and which I'd been unable to hide from her), she wanted to be prepared for them before she saw them.

"Mama," she said hopefully, "he smiling?" I shook my head no as I showed her the photos of the solemn-faced child. She studied them intently. My sister and I weren't the only ones who noticed he had grown. Jaclyn said, "Mama, how big he now?"

She had insisted for a long time that he was only two. She kept careful track of his age in China and did not believe me when I said that he was now three because he'd had a birthday. "There no such thing as birthday in China," she said emphatically, confusing the concept of a birthday party with that of age. I told her again that he was three years old. She was crestfallen.

"But Mama, I want him be little again. I want to carry him again. I want to hold him. I can't carry three years old. That too big for me." Like a mother lamenting the loss of her child's babyhood, Jaclyn wanted to turn back time and recapture all that she had missed.

She then studied the picture of him perched high on a wall more carefully.

"Mama," she said with worry in her voice, "how he get up there? Who put him there?" And then, after a pause, "Who take care of him now?"

"I think your former teacher takes care of him now," I said in a reassuring tone. She shook her head in denial.

"I tell you who take care of him now," she said softly. *"No one."*

I knew her well enough now not to attempt reassurance. My words would ring hollow with her and only provoke a stalemate between us. After all, she knew the truth of that world better than I did.

It won't be long now, Xiao Mei Mei, I silently pleaded, hoping that somehow the power of my thoughts would make their way to his little spirit. Don't be afraid. A whole new life awaits you. One of lunch and toothbrushes, your own clothes and toys, bikes and even towels. We're coming, sweet boy.

Chapter Twenty-one

The Promise Fulfilled

But first, you must believe.
—Unknown

Our last few days before leaving for China were a whirlwind of activity. Prior to the finalization of the referral for Xiao Mei Mei, all we had ever heard from Jaclyn was "He a good boy" and stories extolling his goodness and his sweetness. Now she got the new mom-to-be aside to subtly give her some new information.

"Aunt Lola, I no want Xiao Mei Mei sleep in my bed," she said.

"Why not?" said Laura in surprise, as Jaclyn had talked longingly of sleep-overs with him for months.

"Because he peep the bed at night," Jaclyn whispered. Thanks for the heads-up, kid. Laura promptly bought pull-up diapers just in case he hadn't outgrown this.

Unbeknownst to me, Jaclyn had a secret stash of all her birthday money; she carefully placed it in her backpack. "I have to bring all my money to China," she said to me. "I want buy things for Xiao Mei Mei there." Touched by her generosity, as she had never spent any of her money on herself, I reassured her that we would buy him things when we got there.

"No, Mama," she said. "Not *you* buy things. I want buy things myself for my baby." Then she revealed the real reason behind her desperate desire to shop: "When he sad because he don't like his new mama, I give him things I buy." Bribery; it was our tried-and-true strategy.

On our last day at home, Rick, who was remaining behind with the other two kids, hugged her close and teased her by saying, "Are you sure you want to go, Jaclyn? I'll miss you so much."

"Yes, Daddy," she said solemnly. "You can kiss my picture if you miss me. I have to go to China and get my baby. He wait a very long time."

Then Jaclyn asked me, "Mama, do you know what we are going to do after we get my baby?" I shook my head no and braced myself for the answer. She smiled her brilliant smile and said, "PARTY!" Yes, we would party. On that day we would celebrate the good. We would celebrate Jaclyn's unspoken promise to this child to find him a mama. We would savor the moment. We would take the time to marvel at the series of events that had worked together to reunite these two children who clung to each other when they had no one else. We would celebrate his life. We would celebrate all the lives that had made this day possible. We would celebrate those who pledged, those who prayed, those who met our needs without asking, those who held us when we cried, those who worked through the system, those who begged on our behalf, those who heard and acted, and finally, those who shared our joy.

At the airport we met the Bauers, who were traveling with us to Gualing for a seven-month-old boy. They showed us their referral picture, and then Laura proudly reciprocated by showing hers. Jaclyn took her to task for saying it was a photo of her baby. "It MY baby," she said in annoyance.

Laura then said wisely, "Yes, of course he is your baby. But you are going to share him with me, right?" Jaclyn was appeased.

We landed in Beijing and began the tourist circuit early the next morning. On the bus between tourist attractions, Jaclyn sat down for a little chat with my boss, Mary. Jaclyn began by peppering her with personal questions as I slunk down in my seat in embarrassment. Mary, now a superintendent but formerly a kindergarten teacher, took it all in stride and did not flinch from Jaclyn's inquisitiveness. Mary is diminutive in size, with warm brown eyes and a ready smile. Jaclyn was enchanted with her easy manner and, like any child, didn't know to be intimidated by Mary's important position.

Maybe because of Mary's openness with her, Jaclyn, in a supreme act of trust, began to tell Mary about her life in the orphanage. It was the first time she had shared her story with anyone outside our immediate family. But maybe she had another motive in telling Mary about the deprivation she had suffered. At the end of her discourse, she added a question: "Why you not get one?" she asked, laying a guilt trip on Mary. "We need bring all the kids to America. It a bad place here." We're working on it, Jaclyn, I said silently. One child at a time.

She continued to be full of apprehension. She refused to speak to the Chinese who tried to engage her in conversation, and recoiled from those who tried to touch her. But she did not have the anger I had seen in her on our last visit.

"Do we have tickets home, Mama?" she queried me several times a day. "How many tomorrows till we go back to our regular house?" she asked over and over, followed by her most pressing concern, "How many tomorrows till I get my baby?"

When I tried to call her Jiao, her former Chinese name, which we often used interchangeably with Jaclyn at home, she promptly corrected me by saying that she wanted to be called Jaclyn.

"This not MY China," she said. "I America girl now."

On our second morning Jaclyn told me, for the first time ever, that she had had a bad dream. "I dream Xiao Mei Mei fall in deep hole. I can't get him. I need big stick get him out. I not have big stick," she said sadly. The meaning of the dream was clear: she was afraid, now that we were this close, that he would somehow fall from her grasp or be beyond her reach.

Jeff knelt at her side and reassured her. "I'd get a big stick, Jaclyn," he said soothingly. "We won't leave him here. Nothing will happen to him now."

And in spite of her fears, I knew that on this day, now that we had finally arrived in Gualing, the promise would be fulfilled.

It was never a promise spoken in words. I remembered Jaclyn's story of the last day she lived at the orphanage. After Xiao Mei Mei had studied her photo book of her new family for the umpteenth time, he had asked her if he could come to live with her. But she did not promise. Even when we returned to Gualing to visit him, she did not promise. Jaclyn, ever mindful of her baby's feelings, knew that the ache of false hope had the power to devastate more than anything else in the dark place where he waited. Maybe she knew it was better not to dare hope at all. But it was a promise nonetheless, a sacred vow she made, at some level deep in her soul, to herself. She would help her baby "find a mama." And she would not be dissuaded.

Today was the day. The promise would be fulfilled.

Jaclyn carefully picked out her favorite dress for the big day. After all, first impressions are everything. Mary teased her by saying, "Jaclyn, do you think today we should go to the museums and see stuff?"

"OK," Jaclyn replied agreeably, "but I have to get my baby first." She knew it was finally the day. "As soon as you see him, Jaclyn, you can go to him," I said. "You don't have to wait any longer." She had waited so long for this moment, I didn't want her to have to wait on ceremony. "I not get in trouble with the teacher?" she asked, her brow furrowed in worry.

"You can run if you want to," I assured her. "I'll make sure no one stops you." As if anyone could.

"Aunt Lola," Jaclyn asked, "you got clothes for Xiao Mei Mei? You got toys for him?" Laura showed Jaclyn all she had brought so that she wouldn't worry.

"Today Xiao Mei Mei get a family!" Jaclyn said, beaming, to anyone who would listen.

Because I knew that Jaclyn got very upset when I cried, I tried to explain to her that today Mommy would be crying tears of joy and that she was not to be upset by them. "I no understand what you saying," she said over and over in frustration as I tried to explain. She could not comprehend how tears would have any place on such a happy occasion.

We proceeded to the new Office of Civil Affairs. It was in a huge, modern high-rise building and was so new that the chairs were still covered in plastic. It was a stark contrast to the former digs that we had visited on previous trips. The minutes we waited seemed like an eternity. Finally we heard a rustle in the hall. The Bauers' baby was coming.

And then, before we knew it, Xiao Mei Mei was standing in the doorway. He stopped walking, frozen in terror.

"There he is!" Jaclyn squealed happily. She went to him and gently stroked his cheek; tears ran down it. She took inventory. She checked out his fresh new haircut, carefully checked his fingers and wiped his tiny hand. She made sure that this time his shoes were on the right feet. She seemed satisfied that he looked well cared for.

Jaclyn stretched out her hand, as I did when I met her so long ago, and Xiao Mei Mei clasped it firmly. The circle was complete. Each mother had claimed her child.

Xiao Mei Mei never took his eyes from her face, even when his new dad got close to him. Jeff brought out the potato chips that had so successfully won over Willow on our last trip, and Xiao Mei Mei was taking potato chips from his dad's outstretched hand in no time. After he had a few, Jaclyn went to Laura. "He need a drink now," she prompted.

He had some tears, but not nearly the trauma that often accompanies this first meeting. The teacher, the kind young woman who had also cared for Jaclyn, had tears in her eyes as she watched. She and I, talking through our guide, Joan, also had a good chuckle. I told her how happy Jaclyn was in America, but also told her what an active little girl she was.

"Yes, I know!" She laughed. "She was like that here, too!"

"Why didn't you warn me?" was my retort, which brought on a burst of giggles from her. We showed her pictures of Jin Xun Li with her new American family; she reveled in them. No one could ever convince me that this gentle soul, like so many others that worked in these Chinese orphanages, didn't love these kids.

The teacher had a letter in her hand that she explained to me by saying, "Last year a mother came here very concerned about this little boy. She was desperate to keep a connection with the child that her daughter had loved so much. She entrusted me with this envelope that contained information about how to contact her. It also had a picture of the two children together. She begged me to give it to his adoptive parents. I have carefully held on to it all this time. When I heard that he was to be adopted, I brought it with me to give to his new family."

Then she paused, seeing my confused expression, and smiled while saying, "And that mom was you!"

I had forgotten all about the letter. I marveled at the series of events that had led to its return; I would treasure it always. "I cannot believe that the officials in Beijing have allowed this second identified adoption in your family," the teacher continued on. "Nearly all identified adoption attempts, those where a specific child was requested, had been denied at our orphanage in the past year." Her words confirmed what I already knew: we had been incredibly blessed.

Jaclyn touched Xiao Mei Mei's cheek and whispered to him, "You got a family." He did not understand her words of comfort, but he did not let go of her hand. The comfort of her touch he knew.

I had worried that because he was so young, because so much time had passed, he would not remember her. She must have secretly worried about the same thing. She asked him earnestly, "You remember Jiao Jiao?" employing her old Chinese nickname in hopes of prompting his memory. Of course, he could not understand the question spoken in English, but the eyes locked on her face were answer enough.

Mary still crouched near the doorway, taking pictures but mostly watching the reunion in riveted fascination. Tears welled in her eyes as she struggled to find words to convey the emotion that we all felt.

Unlike most children, frozen in terror, their words painfully locked inside on this first day, Xiao Mei Mei spoke early on. First he told us that he had to go to the bathroom, and then, in confusion about where he was, he asked if he could go outside and play on the swing. (There was one swing in the courtyard of the orphanage.) But I was sure now that Jaclyn had truly forgotten her Chinese words; if anything had brought them back, it would have been this chance to speak to her baby again. Sadly, she could not understand him, and relied on our guide to interpret, as we did. Although we did not understand the words, the pitch and tenor of his tiny voice were darling. It was music to our ears.

We moved on to the photo shop to complete the next task in the process, to have a family picture taken for the Chinese government records. I knelt next to Jaclyn while we waited and asked her, "Are you happy, Jaclyn?"

"Yes, I happy. I have my baby now," she said quietly. And then, as she contemplated this further, the toughest, bravest little soul I know lost it. Really lost it. I looked over and saw the tears start; they quickly escalated into deep, choking sobs.

In this most improbable of places, I sat down on the dirty stone steps in the front of the shop and held her in my lap. She wrapped her arms and legs around my torso as if she were an infant. Her wails could be heard by all who passed by on the street, but I had no consciousness of them. All my thoughts were about her. How much I wanted to rid her of these demons. But they were not mine to vanquish; they were hers alone. I didn't have the power to wring this grief from her.

And so she cried in the way she did for months after I first adopted her, in a nearly catatonic state, with no sense of her surroundings. All the pent-up worry, all the grief, all the fear, all the longing came tumbling out in sobs of relief. Waves of tears flooded her and carried away her sorrow. She cried as she had never cried before. I couldn't stand to feel it. The only thing that made it bearable was knowing that it was over. The time for tears was finally over. I held her while she cried it all out, stroking her hair, patting her back, holding her tightly against my body, reassuring her over and over that her baby was safe now and that it would be all right.

She cried until she was spent. She cried until she had no tears left. I thought of the irony that she now knew what it was to cry those inexplicable "happy tears." But it was also a stark reminder of something I often forgot: she was, after all, barely five years old herself.

Once she regained some semblance of control, Jaclyn continued to coach the moms. "You baby got face all messy on his mouth. You have to wipe it," she instructed Julie Bauer. Their baby, Jason, was a robust, healthy little guy who had been all smiles from the start and looked, incredibly enough, as often happens in adoption, just like his dad.

Jaclyn also told Laura, "Xiao Mei Mei need go potty first. Then bath. Then we play. Then we have lunch." And this turned out to be the schedule.

Xiao Mei Mei clutched Jaclyn's hand and his new dad's as we made our way back to the hotel. The first instinct for adoptive parents is to bathe the child and by doing so take inventory of his physical condition. But the first undressing was always a trauma. There is a sense of vulnerability inherent in losing one's clothing. To my surprise, Xiao Mei Mei's instinct when Jeff undressed him was to cry out, "Mama."

He had on girl's underpants that looked to be about twelve sizes too big. We all laughed when Jeff yelled out from the bathroom, "It's a *boy!*" When he was naked, a matchstick of a child stood staring back at us. He was skeletal in size, his skin the pasty white color of those who lack vitamins, nutrients, and sunshine as a regular part of their lives. Jaclyn went potty with him to show him how the toilet worked and also got in the tub with him for her second bath of the day.

The tub bubbles brought out the first smile; that is, after he got over his fear of them. And what a smile! He had dimples! We had a bet going on how long it would take to see his first real smile. None of us would have believed that it would happen in less than three hours.

At the hotel restaurant Jaclyn said, "I want him sit by my lap." He reached his hand to her when he wanted a roll, and she gently buttered it and broke it into pieces for him. She helped him with his juice. He sat on Jeff's lap and let him assist, too. Lunch was full of happy smiles as his dad played with him. Jaclyn begged to share his bed tonight, and his parents happily gave their permission. She was still sorting out the roles; she was a blend of both mother and child, but was generous in allowing the adult parents to play their rightful roles.

Back in the hotel room, Jaclyn helped him open his new backpack, which was stuffed with toys. The kids sat on his cot and had a ball playing together. Jaclyn delighted in showing him all his new stuff while asking solicitously, "You like it?" Xiao Mei Mei loved all his toy cars and boisterously raced them across the bed.

He and Jaclyn rolled over each other like puppies, shrieking with joy. Jaclyn scolded him when he started playing with the phone and was shocked when he didn't obey her stern commands to "stop." Although he didn't recognize the word, her tone was clearly one of disapproval. And he couldn't have cared less. Jaclyn seemed mystified by what had happened to the compliant toddler she once knew.

We didn't stray from the hotel room all afternoon and decided to head out for an early dinner at the hotel next door. By the time we arrived, Jaclyn was so spent from the emotion of the day that she fell asleep on the table.

Later, as the children readied for bed, Jaclyn was very upset that Xiao Mei Mei didn't have a teddy bear to sleep with. I showed her the one that Mary had bought him, but she was frustrated by my inability to understand what she meant.

"No, Mama, this one," she said, showing me the picture of him at the orphanage when we visited him last year and she brought him a teddy bear.

"It seems as if he doesn't have that teddy bear any longer," I said to Jaclyn. It confirmed for her what she had feared in her heart all along, that the other child who had snatched it from him as soon as she left had never been made to give it back to its rightful owner.

"That why you can't bring things to China," she said sadly.

Jeff woke in the night and checked on his new son. Xiao Mei Mei and Jaclyn were holding hands in their sleep, just like old times.

To say that we were all doing well at the end of that first day doesn't even begin to capture it. What a privilege it had been to share this day. How I thanked God for this day of happy tears.

Chapter Twenty-two

A New Beginning

A boy is Truth with dirt on its face, Beauty with a cut on its finger, Wisdom with
bubble gum in its hair and the Hope of the future with a frog in its pocket.
—Alan Beck

As the days passed, things could not have gone more smoothly. In fact, Xiao Mei Mei had not cried since our first meeting. I wished I could say the same for Jaclyn. On this trip I heard even more stories about her life at the orphanage. When she finally fell asleep, she was plagued by bad dreams. She cried and whimpered in her sleep all night. When I questioned her in the morning, she would stoically say: "Something bad happen to Jack-win."

In spite of it all, she continued to mother Xiao Mei Mei, and these instincts finally brought out some of the Chinese language that she claimed to have forgotten. She reacted in alarm by telling him to "stop" in Chinese when he tried to touch something hot. She also asked him if he wanted a drink in Chinese.

He was now, after all, three years old and clearly no sissy, so he would stubbornly ignore her calls of "Xiao Mei Mei" (little sister), much to her frustration. She scolded Mary when she called him that; it was Jaclyn's exclusive pet name for him, not to be used now by others. Reluctantly she shifted to calling him "Xiao Dee Dee" (little brother) or Xiao Xiao, a term of endearment, which he would answer to.

She was still baffled by some of his refusal to obey. She would look at him in dismay as he giggled impishly while dunking his french fries in apple juice, not at all dissuaded by her scolding. We chuckled at these expectations of obedience from a child so inherently mischievous herself.

Xiao Mei Mei loved playing with all his new toys. He lined up all his Matchbox cars and especially loved playing with a tiny jeep. Jaclyn continued to scold him when he was too boisterous by saying, "We don't throw toys," but she seemed to delight in his joy.

She was shocked by his new independence. He dressed himself now, used the bathroom without help, and said, "No, no, no," while giggling right back at her after she scolded him. Jaclyn wanted to smother him with hugs and kisses and, like any boy, he pushed her fiercest embraces away with a look that said, "All right. Enough already! I know you're glad to see me, but geez!" They held hands when walking anywhere, or she insisted in pushing him in his "wagon" (stroller).

Jaclyn was crushed on one occasion when she tried to hold his hand. He was holding candy in it, and he instinctively pulled his hand away because he feared she would take it. "But, Mama," she said in a hurt tone, "I *never* take things away from Xiao Mei Mei." She could not understand how he could think otherwise even for a moment.

He showed no signs of the food anxiety that we had seen in both Jaclyn and Willow. He loved his first ice cream bar after Jaclyn showed him how to eat it. However, he still preferred rice if given a choice.

Mary, on the other hand, had basically stopped eating. Given that she currently weighed about a hundred pounds, I was worried about how long she was going to survive on a few spoonfuls of white rice at each meal. We took her to dinner at the restaurant next door to our hotel and trusted Jeff to order. The menu choices included:

- Stewed caterpillar fungus with quail
- Fried duck chin
- Sucking pigeon hot pot with ginger
- Stewed goose feet
- Stewed swallow's nest in orange (also in other flavors)
- Chaozhou goose stomach in marinated sauce
- Steamed fish head with wild chili
- Goose head with beam [*sic*] sauce
- Roast preserved muntijac in shred (a kind of wild animal, the menu said)
- Steamed polished glutinous rice in palm leaf
- Banana egg
- Overcooked pig leg
- Cool stirred ox leg skin
- Stir-fried pot-stewed pieces of intestine

As Mary visibly paled, I assured Jeff that caterpillar fungus was one of her favorite dishes. I dug into the deep-fried grasshopper and then proudly announced I was ready to audition for *Survivor*.

Xiao Mei Mei carefully picked up the crumbs of food left on the table after eating and placed them in his bowl to eat. Laura burst into tears the first time she saw this. He had known want. He was her child. How could she not grieve about this?

The new, richer diet had upset his stomach, and he vomited. Afterward, he cowered, sure he would be punished, as Jaclyn said this was one of the big "no-no's" in the institution. After some time, and much assurance that he was not going to be punished, he reverted back to his old self.

I had thought that all this might be bittersweet for me since I had thought so many times about his being my son, but it was not. I had pictured myself swallowing hard and putting on a happy face for my sister, but it was not that way at all. I was so happy for him, for Laura and Jeff, and most of all for Jaclyn, my heart was so full so joy, that there was no room left for regret.

Every time we had seen him before, he had been so sad.

"Does he ever smile, Jaclyn?" I had asked.

"No, Mama," she said sadly. Well, the kid who never smiled before couldn't stop smiling now. His dimples were always poking through. He delighted in everything. He giggled. He ran. He teased. He played. He laughed. He loved.

Laura could not believe how smoothly the transition was going. "I'm so in love. He's so *special*. This has been so easy," she said over and over. And how could she have thought anything else? Didn't Jaclyn tell us all along, "He a good boy"? As in all things, she spoke the truth.

When he readied for bed the second night he said with a smile, "Xie xie, Jiao Jiao. Wo ai nee." (Thank you, Jaclyn. I love you.)

This time, I didn't even try to stop the happy tears.

Xiao Mei Mei's antics were so adorable, it was hard to try to scold him. Jaclyn continued to be surprised by his behavior. "I no like Xiao Mei Mei not listen to his daddy," she said in a huff.

"Well, you don't always listen to yours, Jaclyn," I said with a teasing smile. But her puzzlement seemed to say, "I raised you better than that!"

"Maybe we should have considered the source when she said he was 'a good boy,' " Mary said with a chuckle.

We took the children to the zoo, and Jaclyn soon tired of walking. Sickened by the primitive conditions of the cramped cages and the filth the animals were forced to wallow in, I was happy when Jaclyn insisted that we go to the nearby playground instead. We agreed to meet everyone back at the entrance in an hour.

The playground was deserted and filled with colorful climbing equipment. Jaclyn had no sooner begun to explore than, for no apparent reason, an irate and officious-sounding attendant appeared and scolded us menacingly and shooed us away. After she left, I was determined to sneak back in, but Jaclyn was too intimidated by the potential presence of another Chinese authority figure to follow.

"The police come!" Jaclyn said in terror.

So instead we sat on a nearby bench waiting for the others to return. There were several sidewalks nearby, and I noticed Jaclyn carefully watching the children that were walking alone. She pointed to several of them and asked with concern, "Where their mama?" The issue of abandonment surfaced regularly here.

While we sat quietly people-watching, I noticed that Jaclyn had turned pensive. "What are you thinking about?" I queried gently. Nothing could have prepared me for her response.

"I see ladies who look like my China mama," she said. I swallowed hard. "What did she look like, Jaclyn?" I asked.

"She got long hair. She tall. She pretty," was Jaclyn's response. This was the first time I heard her say something kind about her birth mother. I hugged her tight and said, "I know how much she must miss you, Jaclyn."

"She not miss me!" Jaclyn responded furiously. "She not like me!"

"Oh, Jaclyn, there's no way that someone could know you and not love you."

"I no want to go China again ever! I no want to come here when I big! I want to stay in America always," she said firmly with no traces of her earlier anger.

"That's fine, Jaclyn, if that's what you want. You don't need to ever come back to visit," I replied. What a change, I thought, from the little girl who chafed at the bit, asking for months when we could go to China to get her baby. Clearly, though, she'd had only one purpose in mind.

After asking for permission, through our guide's interpretation, and receiving his assent, Laura and Jeff now started to call Xiao Mei Mei by his American name, Lee. He intrigued everyone we met. A boy being adopted was a rarity, and the Chinese everywhere wanted to touch him, to speak to him, to pinch his cheek.

When Laura or Jeff moved away from the table, the shy Chinese waitresses would swarm around him and cluck over him. Lee conversed freely with them and answered their questions. He was not the shy, pathetic little victim we'd anticipated; he was very self-confident and knew what he wanted. His infectious giggle and warm smile charmed everyone who met him.

He had definitely started bonding with his new family and seemed to be a guy's guy. He loved riding on his daddy's shoulders, and he lifted his hands up to Jeff to be carried. He was very jealous if Jaclyn was on Jeff's lap, so the two little ones teased each other about this, too.

Lee had a new favorite toy—the toilet. He flushed it any chance he got. I stopped him one morning from dunking his banana in the toilet before biting it. Later I found banana pieces floating in it, proving once again that where there's a will, there's a way.

I treasured my first kiss from him; I was not sure if I had ever had one that was sweeter.

But the question we all secretly wondered about was, Did Lee really remember Jaclyn? He was, after all, so young when she had left. Our guide, Joan, asked him a series of questions, and among them was "Do you remember Jiao Jiao?" Lee's answer was a resounding "YES!"

How could he not? This kind of love would be hard to forget.

Chapter Twenty-three

A Crack in the Wall

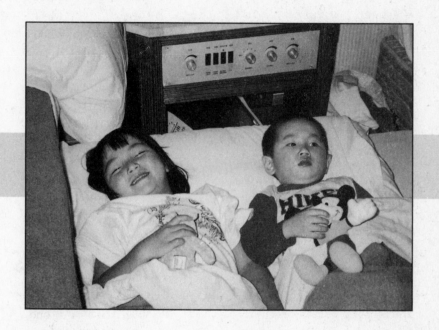

Hope does not ask when the darkness will end. . . . Hope
wonders when the light will begin.
—Susan Squellati Florence

Friday was another sunny, warm day in Gualing. After breakfast we returned to the orphanage for Lee to say his final good-byes. It was wonderful; it was painful.

As the bus pulled down the narrow alley, I strained for the first glimpse of the colorful spires and the bright white-tiled walls. I tried once again to brace myself for what lay beyond the heavy metal gates.

As the bus parked, we noticed that suddenly all the kids with apparent disabilities disappeared from sight; it was obvious that they could not move that fast on their own. In the Chinese manner of saving face, much was still hidden from us. Among the six of us, we saw a lot of discipline—including kids standing with their hands out at their sides as Jaclyn had described and children being slapped on the head.

We walked up the staircase into the open hallways that lined the tiled courtyard. Exposed year-round to the elements, these were the hallways the children and staff traversed to move from room to room. Because our bags of toys and candies had been confiscated the last two times, and because Jaclyn told us that when this happened the kids never ended up with the treats, we tried a covert operation this time. We stuffed our pockets, purses, and backpacks with small toys and candies.

We sneaked into the tiny bedrooms, so filled with beds that there was hardly room to maneuver, and slipped them under the kids' bedrolls when the staff wasn't looking. One member of our group would serve as lookout and distract any staff member approaching the area where the others were hiding the treats. Finally we began to hand them out to the children, who mobbed us, and the staff decided to look the other way. The kids delighted in everything. They thanked us over and over.

The older girls, between the ages of nine and twelve, went to a local school outside the orphanage compound but had returned for lunch. Many of them refused our offer of treats, indicating that we should give them to the younger ones. I marveled at their selfless behavior.

Jaclyn was delighted to greet her old friends and was wonderful about supplying treats to them. She was very proud to do so and not nearly as intimidated this time by the staff, many of whom still remembered her.

We headed down to the rooms that housed the special needs children. The children sat at stark wooden tables, eating small bowls of white rice. Even this task was beyond the ability of some. Rice spilled from the bowls onto the tables and floors. I gave them treats as they finished their lunch. Their obvious needs were hard to witness; they seemed so forsaken.

The staff proudly showed us their plans to expand the playground facilities. Now, several hundred children shared one swing and glider. The tiled courtyard offered no other diversions for their outdoor play. New rooms had been added so that the special needs children would not be warehoused but instead allowed facilities for exercise and play. The facilities had improved yet again since our last visit, so steady progress had been made. I knew this was in no small part due to the financial support they were receiving from adoptive families.

Our gift of handmade baby blankets gave us entrée into the area where the tiny babies were housed. It was the first time I had been permitted to go there. I peered into the open doorways and through the glass windows that lined the corridor. There were more than ninety babies less than six months of age lying two to a crib. The cribs were tiny and painted a soft pale blue.

The nursery was so crowded with cribs that you could hardly move through it. The babies lay almost silently, in the eerie manner of institutionalized children, and many stared blankly off into space. They were swaddled in multiple layers of clothes, as is the Chinese tradition even thought it was a very warm day. Bright new quilts covered them. Several volunteer workers wearing clean white smocks came to the window to show me the babies that they held cradled in their arms.

I stared at their beautiful faces, and tears streamed down my face. A volunteer grabbed my hand and said fervently, "Please, please tell all your friends that we have so many babies here. We *desperately* need families." I wished I could take a truckload with me. I knew it would be easy to find homes for these beautiful children. I promised her I would, and silently railed once again about the endless government paperwork systems that kept these babies here while so many families waited more than a year to gain the necessary approvals to bring them home.

We wandered through the facility, into the various rooms and the courtyard, and were swarmed by children, starved for attention, wherever we went. Mary, still a teacher at heart, loved showing all the curious older boys how her digital camera worked. They laughed out loud when they saw their own faces captured by it.

I tried not to gasp out loud at the faces that were severely bruised. I mourned the children who stared blankly and those who shuffled along with only a barely perceptible lifting of their heads to look at the strangers in their midst. These were the ones who had given up, and their lack of spirit was obvious even to a casual observer. I shuddered when I thought of Jaclyn living in their midst.

As we walked down a corridor, a worker stopped her mopping and rushed over to the children, thrilled almost beyond words to see Jaclyn and Lee together again. "I remember when she lived here, how much she loved him. He was very special to her and she loved him protectively," the worker said. It validated what we knew.

This prompted Jaclyn's old teacher to reminisce with us. "I remember when you sent your disposable cameras before her adoption. I asked Jiao whom she wanted her picture taken with. She said, 'Tan Dong Jin. I want all my pictures with Tan Dong Jin so I can remember him always.' "

In marked contrast to her behavior when we visited last, Jaclyn seemed very comfortable. She didn't cling to me in fear. She seemed to take her cues from Lee, and he acted as if he was cock of the walk. He raced up stairs and down hallways as if he owned the place. As we had been told that he was loved by many of the older children, we were not surprised to see a few of them stop to cuddle him and hold him close. Several children greeted him warmly, and he seemed delighted to talk to them. Jaclyn walked easily among the children that curiously approached her, and imitated our manner of handing a treat to each one.

I watched Jaclyn stand deep in thought as she peered over the half wall in the upstairs walkway and watched the children below. I couldn't begin to imagine what she was thinking. She was disappointed that so few of her old friends were around. She had lived in a group of twenty children, and they had followed the same schedule all day long. By staggering the groups, all the children had access to classrooms, the courtyard, and the TV room. We hoped that they were in school or had been adopted. We didn't dare think of any other possibilities.

We moved down to the office area and gathered in the conference room to meet with the director. She entered the room with a welcoming smile on her face, then gasped in surprise when she recognized me. As a slight bow is the customary greeting in China, I was astonished when she gave me several spontaneous, warm embraces. "You are truly 'the mother of the Gualing orphanage,' " she said with a smile. "I can hardly believe that you are back again! I remember your promise to find a mother for Tan Dong Jin, but I did not imagine he would be in your own family!" And then, consistent with Chinese tradition, she offered this: "You must all be our honored guests at a traditional Chinese dinner tonight. All of the officials from the orphanage will be there." We immediately accepted.

As we were boarding the bus, Jaclyn said, "Mama, I see the girl who took care of me when I little." I had never heard her mention this and was anxious to know which child she was talking about. I ran back inside, leaving the whole bus waiting, dragging Jaclyn along by the hand.

"Show me who she is," I insisted, intent upon capturing this new information about her past with at least a photo.

"Mama, that her," she said while pointing to the retreating figure of a girl of about twelve. I motioned to the child to come over to me and secretly took her picture. It was the same girl who had helped care for Tan Dong Jin after Jaclyn left and who had held him fondly on her lap while we visited.

I shook with emotion when we got outside the gates. I foolishly thought our visit would be easier this time. After all, I had seen the orphanage before. And this time I did not have to leave behind a special child I loved, as I had left Jin Xun Li the first time and Tan Dong Jin the second time. Little did I realize that this did not make it easier at all. I cared about them all.

As honored as we were by the invitation, we were also anxious about our dinner with the orphanage administrators. When we had adopted Christy we had also been invited out to eat with the orphanage staff and government officials. I had been anxious about making a good impression and was terrified that some faux pas on my part would cause the adoption to be revoked; that I would somehow be judged not worthy and as a result would never get my long-awaited baby. I vividly remembered the terror of our meal and how hard it was to stop myself from trembling. I had been so anxious to make a good impression that I ate with feigned relish all the unrecognizable, squirmy things they loaded onto our plates.

Remembering this, I made Mary practice saying, "Yum! Yum!" with a big smile on her face in anticipation of the event, as she was the least adventurous of us all in the food department.

The orphanage sent a van to pick us up, with the young teacher as gofer. The dinner was in a very upscale restaurant. I made the first faux pas of the night by sitting down in a chair that the director did not want me to sit in. Her immediate look of disapproval made me leap from my seat. She quickly ushered me to another chair; she had a fixed seating chart in mind. She had ordered a high chair for Jaclyn, which much to my shock Jaclyn got into with no protest. But she did not cower in the presence of these administrators as she had the last time.

The director did most of the talking for their team. I did most of it for ours. Joan, our guide, barely got a bite of food as she did all the translating.

The Chinese believe that exposure to the elements results in illness for babies so they wrap them in multiple layers of clothing and blankets even in the warm weather. Knowing this, the Bauers were sweating by the end of the meal in their effort to keep their tired baby completely covered by clothes, jackets, and blankets, as the staff scolded them every time he wiggled free.

The food turned out to be wonderful—in fact, it was the best we had. Fish appeared as the main course, and it was very unusual looking—

brown and so crisp that the tail turned upward. The head and eyes were staring up, but it turned out to be delicious.

Mary looked at me in puzzlement after she saw the dish they called corn soup. "What's in there beside corn?" she whispered.

"It's corn soup with big white puffy things," I told her helpfully.

At one point the director leaped from her chair and began toasting Mary. Mary leaped from her chair and toasted her back, which gave us all a good role model to follow when it was our turn to be toasted.

The director scolded Jaclyn early on in the meal for drinking her water before she ate her food, and Jaclyn complied with the Chinese directive and stopped doing so. But I tried to ignore Jaclyn's antics as I sat riveted to the director's words: "When Lou Jiao lived here she was always a very good and helpful girl. She cared for the little ones and was very skilled and adept at it. She told me that she believed that if she was good enough, then she would get a family."

I knew that Jaclyn was always one to speculate about how to work the system, but my heart clenched from hearing this about one so young.

She went on to say, "The orphanage faces many difficult financial challenges. Only one-third of the staff here are paid for by the government, the rest are volunteers. We could not manage without them."

She continued, "But money is only one of the problems. We are desperate for homes for these children, especially the babies and the special needs children. We now have three hundred and eighty children residing here. That is an increase of eighty from when you visited last year. No matter how many adoptions we do, the children still keep coming. Even today a baby was left at the front gate, as was a little girl about six years old." She paused briefly to let her words sink in.

"Always, they continue to come," she said with a weary smile.

She spoke about the system for older child adoptions and made this surprising comment: "I believe that the reason the older children cry when they are adopted is that they want to stay in the orphanage. Often the care here has been better and more consistent than what they knew in their birth families, and they are afraid to trust in a family again. So I tell the staff to be harsh with them at the end so they will want to go."

But the children are not the only ones traumatized by the separation.

"I purposefully do not tell the staff until right before the child leaves that they are being adopted. Based on my ten years of experience here, this makes it easier for all. The staff grieve terribly for the children that they have come to love, and I do not want their tears to make it harder for the children to go."

Jaclyn behaved pretty well through all this, but she was, after all, Jaclyn, so there were a few moments when she reached and grabbed for things rudely or whined and pouted when she could not have her way. The orphanage staff expressed keen disappointment over the fact that she didn't speak Chinese anymore. Not wanting them to think that I didn't value her heritage, I tried to explain that she had been enrolled in Chinese school and still seemed to understand the language but sometimes was a little less than cooperative.

"Yes, I have noticed this behavior," the director said. "You spoil the children in America. We give you well-mannered children, but once the children get families, they become naughty like Lou Jiao." She gave me a pointed glance, not at all concerned that her words would be considered rude. I could hardly deny that Jaclyn's behavior was less than stellar and was not at all upset by the director's gentle rebuke.

This was not the only difference she saw between the two cultures.

"American women carry the babies in the front, not the back like Chinese do. This is because American women don't have to do anything, while Chinese women must work and therefore need their hands free," she said firmly. I wondered with a smile if she thought that parenting Jaclyn, based on what she had seen, was "doing nothing."

At the end of the evening, she turned to Jaclyn and sweetly extended this sincere invitation: "Lou Jiao, the next time you come to visit you will have a special honor! We will save a bed in the orphanage for you to sleep in instead of staying at the hotel." Luckily, Jaclyn did not tell her what she thought of this offer; she simply ignored it. I sighed in relief.

I have heard people suggest that the orphanage administrators are somewhat self-serving, that donations earmarked for other purposes find their way into their own pockets, but when we dropped the director and the assistant director back at their homes after dinner, we saw that they lived in very run-down one-room apartments. These were certainly not the digs that anyone with any extra money would have. I chose to believe that they were good people doing the best job that they could and that we couldn't second-guess their decisions without walking in their shoes. And I knew I couldn't walk in those shoes for a day.

Back at the hotel, I settled Jaclyn down for bed. As I did so, I asked her to tell me more about the older girl who had cared for her. She told me, "I was sick and had to go doctor room. She came and sat by me a long time. She bring her homework and do it next to me." Jaclyn had a far-away look in her eyes as she recalled the time. "She take care of my baby for me while I sick. I not ask her do it. She just do it." Jaclyn smiled then at the memory of this child's kindness to her.

Finally, after so long, she could remember the bright spots, the kind-nesses, the compassion as children reached out to comfort other children. I was thrilled to finally have the gift of her first good memory of her life in the orphanage.

Chapter Twenty-four

Lee's New Life

If I could reach up and hold a star for every time you've made me smile,
the entire evening sky would be in the palm of my hand.
—Unknown

By the end of the second week, I was desperate to be home. I missed my husband and my girls, and I'm ashamed to admit that I missed my life of comfort. But I had begun to realize that the responsibility I felt toward children had blurred the lines in my own life. When I was in China, I felt I was failing in my responsibility to the children under my own roof. When I was home, I felt I was failing in my responsibility to the children who reached their hands out to any stranger who would offer their touch in return. The line where my responsibility for one ended and the other began had almost ceased to exist. And I was not foolish enough to believe that children's suffering existed only in remote corners of the world. I knew the sobering statistics about the land of plenty: in the United States, 14 million children go to bed hungry each night, 4,200 die from gunfire each year, and 1 million suffer from abuse and neglect. What I knew with certainty was they all needed us. We were all collectively responsible for the world's children.

Jaclyn was disappointed by the plane ride home. "Where the angels?" she said as we got above the clouds. "I not see them!" I wondered how she could not, when the one sitting next to me was so clearly visible.

Jeff and I had some opportunities to really talk on this flight, something we rarely make time for, so maybe the long plane rides were really a gift in disguise. "You know that the small inheritance we used to pay for the adoptions came from my aunt, who was, ironically, childless. I'm not sure she would've even understood this purpose," he began. "She'd told me about the bequest, and I'd always planned to use the money to buy a larger house, I was so sure that this was what we needed in order to be happy. How could I have ever thought that any material things could compare to this experience? That the joy in owning could ever come close to the joy in loving?"

So it seemed fitting that this father came bounding off the long flight with his new son perched proudly in his arms. A crowd of family and friends were waiting at the airport to welcome this little one whose presence had been felt for so long among all of us. Balloons and toys were offered from outstretched hands, and some of the older kids held aloft a banner proclaiming "Welcome to America, Lee."

Even jet lag and fatigue could not suppress the ear-to-ear grin of the new dad, previously a father of three girls, as he ripped open a pack of cigars and handed them out while proclaiming joyfully, "It's a BOY!"

My girls came running to me, and I scooped them up while trying to hug Rick, too. Jaclyn, of course, blocked the pack of children rushing forward and protectively put her arms around Lee until he felt comfortable enough to explore on his own. When the melee of hugs had dissipated, Rick and I each held Lee for a few precious moments and exchanged teary glances.

"I love this kid," Rick said, blinking back the tears. A small part of each of us still thought of him as our own; the lines here had blurred, too. We all loved him; we were all collectively responsible for giving him the best future possible.

As I heard the buzz of joyous greetings and saw the circle of love as family and friends surrounded him, I knew that at this moment, something was very right in this world—another one of God's children had found his way home.

But kids do have a way of providing a reality check. Kate, filled with emotion, said, "Mom, do you know why I missed you so much?" I braced myself to hear some loving thoughts. "Because Daddy made us pick up our own clothes!" she said with indignation.

Jaclyn and I made it through the rest of day in an exhausted fog. She decided on her own to go to bed early. I followed her, but this time the familiar apprehension was gone. There would be no more heartfelt pleas to God. I wondered what Jaclyn's new prayer might be.

She put on her Barbie nightgown and wearily crawled into her bed. She closed her eyes and solemnly said, "Dear God, Please let Xiao Mei Mei keep his family. Aunt Lola take care of him now. Now he can play stuff. Amen."

She had closure; Laura was now the mom and she was fine with that. More than fine. We all were.

Two weeks after we returned home, Spence Abraham lost his Senate seat and with it his position as chairman of the immigration committee in the Senate. Shortly after that the Chinese Center for Adoption Affairs passed new rules further restricting identified adoptions. Lee had gotten out just in time.

Even in my clouded, jet-lagged state, I was cognizant of what I needed to do immediately: offer heartfelt thanks to those responsible for helping Lee find his way home. But if I thanked all those who had prayed for him and offered their love and support, my list of thank-you notes would have been endless. So I instead concentrated on the major players in this little saga. I was always remembering the story in Luke 17:12–19 about how Christ healed ten lepers, and nine of them went merrily on their way; only one came back to give thanks. I knew that I was too often guilty of living my life this same way—expecting others to help me and taking their kindness for granted. I purchased small gifts and wrote heartfelt notes of thanks. I made sure that these were in the mail before I attended to any of the other tasks of daily living that clamored for my attention. I was secretly proud of my promptness and the fact that I remembered to make giving thanks a priority.

Rick, who like me had listened to Jaclyn's prayers for her baby for so long now, was as relieved as I was to have these heart-wrenching prayers behind us. On our first day back, he teased Jaclyn by posing this question: "Jaclyn, now what are you going to say to God every night since your baby is finally here?"

Jaclyn, without a moment of hesitation, offered simply this: "I say *thank you!*" And then, with a start, I realized that I had my priorities all wrong. Jaclyn knew that in matters of thanks, you start at the top.

True to her word, Jaclyn did not forget to say thank you. Night after night she would say different versions of this prayer: "Dear God, Thank you and Jesus and Snow White bring my baby here. I love him. I LOVE HIM. I take care of him always. He always be my baby. Now he happy. I give him toys. Now he can play. Amen." I was pretty sure that God had never received more eloquent or heartfelt thanks.

And so I offered this prayer of my own: May she always believe that prayers are answered. May she always believe that dreams can come true. May she always believe that God hears her.

May she always believe.

Jaclyn's sense of humor was still intact.

"We're going to see Lee on Saturday," I told her.

"*Again?*" she replied with mock annoyance, as if this was by now old hat. Then she burst into giggles at the ridiculousness of ever taking these get-togethers for granted.

Every time we saw him, I was amazed by how remarkably well he was adjusting. His first night in his new home he woke in terror, unsure of where he was, and cried fearfully. He was also upset every time his new dad left for work. He had a few bouts of quiet sobbing, not triggered by anything in particular other than having had his whole world turned upside down. Other than these isolated incidents, he was thriving. He was more than thriving—he radiated joy.

As Jaclyn had warned us, he did have one nighttime accident. When Jeff heard noises and got up to investigate, he found the little guy mopping the floor with rags. Lee braced himself for an angry response, and when none was forthcoming he sighed with deep relief.

In spite of having lived so many years surrounded mostly by girls, as he still was now in his new family, he proved to be all boy. His three sisters abandoned all dolls, dress-up clothes, and the Barbie kingdom. Trucks and toy cars were now the toys of choice as the girls were fascinated by his interest in them and eagerly joined in this play. And then the two kinds of play meshed; Matchbox cars were now pushed in doll carriages.

He was intrigued by how everything worked in this new world and watched with fascination amazing things like garage doors that magically opened by pushing buttons. He ran happily, with nary a fear, into all the tunnels at the McDonald's playland and was not at all cowed, as his sisters were, by the bigger boys blocking his way.

Kate said, "Mom, do you know who he reminds me of? Curious George!" Yes, I could see the similarities—even in stature.

He was a kind little soul and amazingly empathetic. He bopped two of his sisters on the head the first day, just to establish domain, I guess, but since that time the rough play had been nearly nonexistent. If anyone in the household was crying or had been scolded, he was the first at their side offering hugs. He was not dismayed if they angrily pushed his love aside; he cheerfully tried again next time. I hoped he got some of this compassion from watching Jaclyn, who was also visibly pained by the grief of others. I was proud of the fact that the harshness of their world did not numb them to the need for love and empathy in any venue.

Jaclyn, who had carefully listened to this explanation a multitude of times herself, told her sisters firmly, "Xiao Xiao can't come spend the night until he used to his new family." Laura lived only a short half-hour drive away, so we knew the kids would have lots of opportunities to see each other.

Jaclyn spoke to him often on the phone, but often her calls were just a pretext for us to check up on him. Laura was generous in indulging us with anecdotes. We hung on every word. She admitted to secretly feeling almost guilty when she was around us about the incredible gift she had been given.

So that the kids could play together, the dads met at a McDonald's halfway between our two homes for a Saturday breakfast. When it was time to go back home, Jaclyn could not bear to leave Lee.

"Can I show Xiao Xiao my house?" she begged her uncle. So they all ended up at our house. Six little girls and the sole boy in the combined clans sat down for lunch later in the day at my kitchen table. Only one smiled sweetly at me and thanked me for lunch, and it was Lee.

I nearly had to pinch myself to believe that the little shadow that had been in my heart for so long was finally sitting in my kitchen. I watched them both, filled with joy and gratitude, and reveled in the moment of realization that just three weeks ago this same animated little soul, now so alive at my table, lived in a drab institution. It was hard to imagine now.

Lee enthusiastically admired Jaclyn's prized ballerina jewelry box and mustered up the same excitement for the Barbie airplane that Kate was eager to show off. He indulged us all when we begged him for kisses.

When he left, Rick was more than a little sad that this precious child didn't live under our roof. I wanted to believe that it was because he missed guy stuff in our girl-filled nest, but the truth was that this kid was just special. We both missed him with an aching gut every day. But the upside was that we now saw Laura's family regularly. We found the time. The bustle of life no longer interfered with our intention to enjoy our kids and their exuberant delight in each other.

He had brought us all closer together. He had made us believe in miracles. He had made us grateful beyond measure.

I thought often of the uncanny circumstances that brought Lee into our lives and wondered what this meant about the future of our adopted children. Why were they the ones whose lives were changed forever? Were they special in some way that transcended our human knowledge? Surely the fact that they were the ones chosen to be here could not be random. Would they, in some small but tangible way, change this world? Or just change our hearts?

My sister finally acknowledged that it was time; Lee could come and spend the night. Rick, Lee's biggest fan, tried to maximize this opportunity.

"I'll go and get him early on Saturday," he said to me. "Then let's secretly pretend he's ours!" I knew he was only half joking. On the designated Saturday morning, Rick tried to feign that it was accidental, but he woke me at 6 A.M., like a kid on Christmas morning. It was still pitch black outside and I burrowed deeper into the covers, certain that at any moment I would hear the sound of little footsteps on the stairs. Rick couldn't lie still, and his dark brown eyes, normally half closed at this early morning hour, were glowing with excitement. He turned on his side and pulled the pillow off my head: "Today Xiao Xiao is coming over!" Of course, this whole visit was for Jaclyn. Yeah, right.

"What are you going to do if Lee cries and won't go with you?" I murmured groggily as he leaped out of bed.

"I won't take him if he cries," Rick said as he pulled on his Saturday navy blue sweats to ward off the early morning chill and ran his hand over the stubble of his heavy beard. Luckily, Lee jumped in the car and went with him happily. The child seemed to sense how dearly we loved him.

Jaclyn, of course, was ready to take charge. "I tell you, Mama, when he hungry," she said in her usual bossy manner. But Lee was not the meek little puppy that used to follow her everywhere. He was not afraid to stand up to her bossiness. He was amazingly self-sufficient and indicated anything that he wanted by first pointing to the object, then to himself, while saying an emphatic "YES!" His parents called to check on him three times. In the first hour.

But contrary to their fears, he was happy. In fact, he had a ball. We took the kids to a magic show. Magic is, of course, a universal language, and he laughed out loud at the antics.

Although she had talked for months of having him sleep in her bed, at the last minute Jaclyn chickened out. "He peep the bed. I remember from China," she said firmly. She was not dissuaded by his new family's testimonial that he was not a bed wetter. Instead, he slept next to her.

In celebration of this special event, Jaclyn removed a special trinket from her Barbie backpack. This was the backpack we took to China when we adopted her. Ever since, it had held her most sacred treasures. Her favorite tights and ruffled panties. Her red sequined purse. Her sparkly nail polish. All the things she cherished too much to use, but simply admired. She used to keep this full backpack at the end of her bed. For a while, when she overheard us talking about someday moving to Florida, it was accompanied by a packed toy suitcase. She explained all this to me by saying that she wanted to be able to grab her treasures quickly in case we left. I tried to reassure her that she was not going anywhere. At some point she must have started to believe this herself, as the backpack was now finally hidden in her closet. I didn't notice when this red-letter day occurred, but I secretly celebrated the fact that it had.

One of the treasures in there was a pin that I wore to China when I adopted her. It had her picture on it and the words *I love Lou Jiao*. I wore it to our first meeting, and somehow she confiscated it after we got home and hid it in her backpack. I believe, at some level, it represented to her the beginning of her new life. She rarely wore it, but for this auspicious occasion she proudly pinned it on her sweater.

All too soon the long-awaited weekend wound to a close. We went up to get Lee's suitcase. "No, no, no!" he said firmly, shaking his head to emphasize his feelings, when he saw the suitcase. Then he pointed to the ground and said, "STAY! Stay Jiao Jiao."

Rick's eyes brimmed with tears. "I'm not going to wrestle him into the car," he said. "I'm not kidnapping another kid against their will ever again." He was remembering our first meeting with Jaclyn. But this time, he didn't want the child to leave either, which only compounded his sadness. I was completely unsure of what to do next.

In a flash, Jaclyn took charge. She knelt in front of Lee and gently took his face in her hands. "Xiao Xiao, when you miss Jiao Jiao too much you look at this," and with that she carefully unfastened her cherished pin from her sweater and pinned it on him. "And remember that Jiao Jiao always love you." With that, she took his hand and gently led him to the door. And he went, trusting as always in her.

Lee touched hearts; there was no denying that. I had always known that some people had that special magic about them. It is often called charisma, but I'd seen it take different forms. My friend Shari had it. It was as if there was a loving glow surrounding her. People were drawn to her warm smile, her southern charm, her kind mannerisms. You just felt good when you were with her.

My husband had it. I used to say that he was a "bum magnet" because he had about him a magnetic force that attracted those in need, those in trouble, those who hurt. When we walked in any city, if there was a soul who was down and out within a twenty-mile radius, they somehow were drawn to him. He invited them to have lunch with him at his fancy corporate dining room; he was not embarrassed. He listened, he counseled, he freely gave what he had. He refused no one. He didn't understand how people like me could look the other way and continue walking. People just knew that they were safe with him.

And Jaclyn's baby had it. When you were with him, you somehow sensed that he was special. Laura took him to the playground and was amazed at how the other children thronged around, eager to play with him. They squealed, too, at his unabashed giggles on the swings. They all wanted to be next in line to ride the teeter-totter or the glider with him. His sisters fought over who could have the privilege of sleeping in his bed. My girls fought over who got to play with him first, who could sit closest to him, who got the most hugs from him. I remembered how the children had all thronged around him at the airport when he came home and rubbed his tiny head, almost as if they were rubbing a magic genie, as if some of the magic would rub off onto them.

He had a minor cardiac condition. Anxious to be sure he was properly monitored, Laura made an appointment with a prominent cardiologist. We've all been to these specialists—men and women who hold life and death in their hands and sometimes forget that playing God doesn't make them God. They're the ones who are overbooked, too busy, and have become calloused by the awesome decisions they have in their power to make.

Lee was to have a series of tests. In spite of his small stature, he was a brave little soul. He still did not have enough understanding of English to know what was going to happen to him in this strange place among all the tubes and wires, but he tried so hard to cooperate, to suck it up, that he bit his lip until it bled. But he never shed a tear. The physician watched all this but did not comment.

The results of the tests were encouraging. His condition was indeed minor. At the end of the visit, overcome by the magic, this highly esteemed man did something unexpected. He gently bent down and placed one of his large hands on each of Lee's cheeks, and then he softly kissed him on the forehead. "I *love* you," he said, quietly trying to contain his emotion.

Then he turned to my sister and said, "Thank you for sharing this miracle with me."

And then came the first of the lessons we learned from Lee. In China, his orphanage preschool did not have enough chairs. Given his tiny stature, he had shared a chair in the back row with another child. Jaclyn said that the child he shared with was one of those who preyed on him, so it was not surprising to see in the photos that Lee had barely one-third of the chair to perch on.

In spite of his uncomfortable seating, he loved school and wanted to go to school now, too. Unfortunately, the local Head Start program was too full to accommodate him, but Laura brought him with her whenever she took her daughter Willow to the class. After a few shy glances, the staff was touched by the magic he brought with him. An opening miraculously appeared.

When Laura picked him up one morning, the teacher cornered her and said, "He's a real handful, isn't he? He isn't at all like his sister." Her heart sank as she braced to hear about his infraction of the rules.

"Today we played the game 'musical chairs.' The rules of the game were carefully explained to the children. When the music stopped the first time, Lee cheerfully plopped himself into the same chair with another child. He was scolded and reminded again what the rules were. The music started again. Again, he ran to share a chair. No matter how many times he was told 'the right way' to play, he insisted on playing his way. In fact, he was quite delighted with himself, even after repeated scoldings."

Under his rules, no one was left without a place to sit. Under his rules, there was room for all. I guess sharing seemed like a small price to pay to accomplish this.

When Lee came home, I knew that the extraordinary circumstances that brought him here could only mean one thing: he was a child that would show us the way. I believed that, for those who were wise enough to learn from a child, he demonstrated "the right way" to play. A place for everyone.

Thanks for the lesson, Lee.

Chapter Twenty-five

Jaclyn's Gift

Thanks be to God for his indescribable gift!
—2 Corinthians 9:15

I made arrangements for our local mayor, who posed as Santa for the kids, to call the girls in early December. Before Jaclyn got to the important task of making her requests, she decided she'd better bring Santa up to speed on the new developments in her life. "My baby here from China," she told him. "He live with my aunt. His name Xiao Xiao."

Luckily, Santa was unperturbed by this news, as if every youngster he talked to had a baby, so when Jaclyn hung up she assured me that Xiao Xiao was on Santa's list. "Everybody on the list!" she said with relief.

Even though she had reassured herself that Santa would not forget Xiao Xiao, later in the evening Jaclyn came to the realization that she had made an oversight in not telling Santa what to bring him. She thought of a way to remedy this. When she said her prayers she added this request, "God, tell Santa to call Xiao Xiao and ask him what he want for Christmas." She did it in the matter-of-fact manner that one reminds one's partner to stop for milk on the way home.

When she was done praying, Jaclyn explained by saying, "It OK, Mama. Santa live up in the sky, too. God, Jesus, and Santa all live up in the sky together. God the boss, so he tell Santa." Glad we have that all sorted out, I thought wryly.

"It only ten days until Jesus' birthday." I was happy to hear her say this; I knew that too often children get caught up in Santa and forget the real meaning of Christmas. Jaclyn continued her reasoning: "That why we get presents. Santa bring Jesus his presents first because it His birthday."

That left her with only one issue.

"Mama," she said, "When God birthday?" Following this train of logic, I guess if we had all this hoopla for Jesus' birthday, we should really go all out when The Boss has his special day.

———

The holiday season, and all that it brought with it, was in full swing. When I was able to stop the bustle for just a moment to sit and reflect, I realized that I had been given an incredible gift this year. It did not come wrapped in shiny paper. It was not neatly tied with a bow. No one waited for it in interminable lines at the mall. It would not cause me to be filled with regret later when the credit card bill arrived. No one spent time circling the mall for a parking spot to buy it. But what joy it brought me!

The giver was Jaclyn. She had often told me that she was poor in China. And, in this context, she made it clear she no longer considered herself to be poor; she had six dollars to her name. She counted her money regularly and had offered the entire bundle to me on more than one occasion. Because I knew she would willingly give me all that she had, the heartfelt offer touched me deeply each time she made it.

She had not worn her tennis shoes in weeks. I finally found out why—they were too small and pinched her toes. I quickly produced a new pair. Jaclyn sat with me while I rushed to thread the laces so I could send her out the door in them. When we finished putting them on, I checked the toes for fit, then hurried her on her way. She would not be rushed. Instead, she grasped my hand gently and looked directly into my eyes with her intense gaze.

"Thank you, Mama, for shoes," she said simply. Touched by the sincerity of her words and her heartfelt look, I stopped my hurrying. How could I have forgotten that this was a child who never took things for granted?

My other children lost their mittens so many times over the course of the winter that I had developed a new strategy. At the start of the season, I bought five pairs in identical sizes and colors. This way, a pair was not ruined if only one mitten was missing. And I considered myself lucky if even one intact pair was left at the end of the winter. I was clueless about where the others went.

Jaclyn had never lost a mitten. She had one pair that she adored. They were a gift from her beloved Nana, who knew her taste well. They were bright pink with froufrou cuffs; they clashed nicely with her purple and green coat. I had to mend them twice, as they were now on their second winter. The second time, I thought about simply tossing them out and buying new ones. Wasn't it crazy to be mending a five-dollar pair of mittens? But because Jaclyn cherished them so, I found I could not.

Unlike my other two, Jaclyn never misplaced her hat either. It was bright purple with two earflaps. Jaclyn, always a trendsetter, refused to wear it with the flaps over her ears. Instead, she turned it upside down and wore it with one ear flap carefully sticking up over her forehead, the other one in back; it gave her kind of a Russian flair. So when the other two scrambled each morning to find gloves and hats and scarves, Jaclyn always produced hers from the safe place she had left them.

And then I found out why. The last winter Jaclyn spent in China was unusually cold. Snow fell in her city, which was nearly an unheard-of occurrence. Jaclyn remembered it vividly.

"I have coat in China," Jaclyn said, "but I no have mittens or hat or scarf. I touch the snow with my hands." She trembled at the memory as she demonstrated pulling her hand quickly back. "I so cold all the time." Yes, this was a child who would never lose her prized mittens.

Old habits die hard, and I still noticed her surreptitiously inventorying Lee whenever she saw him. So far she had no complaints about the care his new mother was providing. On his last visit, Jaclyn had pinned him to the ground behind the couch so she could smother him with kisses. He was valiantly trying to wiggle free, but I could not find it in my heart to scold her for her overzealous behavior. The miracle that he was here was still too new to be taken for granted. Instead, I had to steel myself against kissing his sweet face with the same fervor. Her gratitude was matched only by my own.

Her tenaciousness with God had now taken a new direction. Her endless pleas for her baby had been replaced by her grateful thanks. And then I heard her thank God fervently for something else: "Thank you, God, for Snow White find me new family."

It gave me great pause. I was sure that I had never thanked God for having a family. I had always taken for granted that a family was my birthright. Aren't we all entitled to at least this? In fact, not only did I take my family for granted, but I was ashamed to admit how many times I had secretly railed about their shortcomings and the times they had disappointed me. I had complained, under the stress of all the holiday gatherings, about the burden of too much family. How could I have been so misguided? I had a family. I belonged to somebody; in fact, I belonged to lots of "somebodies." I had a mother, a father, sisters, and a brother and all the wonderful extended family that they have brought with them through marriage. They loved me. I loved them. How could I never have thanked God for a family?

And so, my greatest gift this year was the gift of gratitude.

Still, on some days the endless demands of the holiday season on a working mother made it difficult to be grateful. I determined that my mantra this year would be "Rejoice! We will spend Christmas with Jaclyn's baby." No matter what happened, I would focus only on the incredible joy that this new addition had brought to our lives, the miracle that he was finally here among us, and the love that united our family. In hindsight, it was a good thing I had that to hold on to.

The joy began with the annual putting up of the Christmas tree. Given how long I had to nag Rick to perform this task, I can only conclude that he would rather be poked in the eye with a stick than tackle this job. Luckily, it was made easier by the fact that he had not yet gotten around to putting away the box from last year.

Our tree was made in China. I thought of the irony of Buddhists working in a Christmas tree factory. Did they puzzle over what they were making and why anyone wanted a fake tree? The branches were coded for simple assembly with letters of the alphabet; when we bought it we figured this would make it a snap to assemble. Once we got home we realized that the assembly did not proceed in alphabetical order. If the directions were misplaced, an annual occurrence at our house, it was nearly impossible to determine the right order. We reached a new record this year in the number of times the tree fell over while being assembled: four.

I had no idea where all the joyful children lived that I saw depicted on TV, who actually loved to decorate the Christmas tree. Mine ran at the first glimmer of anything that seemed remotely like work. Maybe they just noticed how much fun Rick was having as he said very un-Christmassy words under his breath while wrestling the tree into the stand; they wanted no part of it. And in the stampede to get away, my favorite angel ornament was trampled. So I decorated alone while repeating to myself: "Rejoice! We will spend Christmas with Jaclyn's baby."

Two days before Christmas, I set out to do the grocery shopping for the festivities. I grabbed with glee the only parking spot available in the snow-covered lot. When I came out later with two carts of groceries and my three-year-old, Christy, I discovered why that spot had been unclaimed: there was no way to get the cart anywhere near the car. I carried twenty bags of groceries while slipping and sliding over a two-foot snowbank. And silently repeated my mantra while doing so.

Our shopping adventure next led us to the drugstore for more cold medicine. I'd had the same cold since October. I had not slept a night in months. I hacked, I sniffed, I snorted, I got up to blow my nose all night long. It was a typical Michigan winter, a never-ending cold and flu season. In the drugstore Christy insisted on having her own basket to carry. I thought this was adorable, as she could barely hold it. I had no idea that, as she dutifully followed along behind me, she was carefully selecting items to fill her basket. By the time I noticed, she had selected depilatories, bubble bath, suppositories, sparkly nail polish, and mustache wax. There was no persuading her to relinquish the items. I even tried to negotiate by offering to buy her the sparkly nail polish. She was not giving up the suppositories. So a true battle of the wills broke out as we headed to the checkout line.

The clerk was obviously seasonal help and new on the job. Either that or he was a true masochist who enjoyed the torment of seeing how slowly he could ring up twenty items while a small child howled, "IWANTMYBASKET!IWANTMYBASKET!" I silently said to myself, "Rejoice! We will spend Christmas with Jaclyn's baby."

I got home and began to put the household in some semblance of order. My husband had been frozen into inertia by his inability to determine even where to start. I had hoped that by hosting the family Thanksgiving extravaganza, I would be spared Christmas duty. But a family wedding resulted in out-of-town guests. Out-of-town guests whom my husband sheepishly admitted he had invited to stay with us. We did "scissors, paper, rock" to determine which of us would now be sleeping in the Cinderella sleeping bag on the floor.

I went upstairs to clean the bathroom and discovered that some little soul had drawn a green pig with neon marker on the bathroom vanity. When I collared the likely artist, Jaclyn squealed out that Christy had done it. I examined the artwork again, determined that it was beyond Christy's ability, and scolded Jaclyn again. Of course, the pig drew attention away from the big problem in that room: a big, bright orange stain in the middle of the floor. Jaclyn had put on nail polish last weekend. This was the end result. I repeated silently to myself, "Rejoice! We will spend Christmas with Jaclyn's baby."

"Jaclyn, you have been so naughty this year I KNOW Santa is going to bring you coal," Kate said as I eavesdropped. Jaclyn looked at her in confusion.

"I no know what coal is?" she said.

"It's black, and it goes in your stocking if you are bad!" Kate continued.

"I not understand what you saying," Jaclyn sniffed. "Besides, Mama love me all the time. Mama love me even if I bad!"

She knew this. She really knew this. How glad I was that she finally understood the unconditional nature of my love. This was the greatest gift I could ever bestow on her; it was her birthright. The birthright of every child.

A friend told me that there are three phases to Christmas: you believe in Santa, you don't believe in Santa, and you are Santa. On Christmas Eve day, my husband sheepishly asked at 7:30 A.M. if I could "find" a gift for a friend's daughter he was on his way to visit. What does this man think, I silently railed, that I'm an elf with a little workshop behind the house? I carefully orchestrated more than a hundred gifts each holiday season; I had yet to "find" one. I dug through the closets looking for anything plausible while sighing deeply and repeating to myself, "Rejoice! We will spend Christmas with Jaclyn's baby."

Jaclyn's baby seemed to have brought out the spirit of the season in others, too. After two adoptions in one calendar year, finances were tight at my sister's home. Added to this, her four children, all under the age of six, had been sick almost continually for a month. The previous week, three of them had strep throat and scarlet fever simultaneously. She had been literally homebound.

The doorbell rang, and standing there was a woman she had never met before. The woman had known need herself at holiday times in the past and had heard the story of Jaclyn's baby. She handed my sister a huge box. Inside were five Christmas gifts for each of her children, stocking stuffers, gift wrap, tags and bows, and even a gift for the adults. A complete Christmas for the entire family. The relief in knowing that this burden had been lifted from her filled Laura with such emotion that she burst into tears.

Another good Samaritan left a big holiday ham on their doorstep. The gifts continued to arrive. In the adoptive community, the story of Jaclyn's baby had spread like wildfire. One of Lee's fans lived in Tennessee. She made it her mission to dress him, and dress him she did. Boxes kept arriving filled with her son's hand-me-downs from all the best kid's stores. Lee quickly proved to be a clotheshorse. When the boxes arrived, he dove into them headfirst, joyfully exclaiming, "This-a mine? THIS-A MINE!" How it made my heart soar to know that so many shared my mantra of rejoicing.

After unwrapping her Christmas gifts, Jaclyn put one aside.

"I want give this to my baby," she said and was not dissuaded by my assurance that we had many other gifts for him; she needed for it to be from her.

But she was a little disappointed in Santa. Unbeknownst to me, she had secretly told him that she needed a pink vanity to sit at while applying her makeup. When it was not under the tree, she refused to believe her wish had not been granted. She ran downstairs and all over the house to look. Later, she shrugged and said to me, "It will come in the mail."

Yes, wishes did come true in her world. If it was possible for her wish for her baby to be granted, surely a small thing like a pink vanity was not too much to hope for.

As we sat down at the holiday table, Rick began with a prayer of thanks. Jaclyn was not satisfied with the solemn Christmas blessing. She piped up with, "MY turn!" Then she exuberantly said, "Dear God, please watch over my baby. I *love* him! I LOVE HIM! Amen."

Lee was oblivious to all the fuss. Like any small boy, he dug into the gifts with enthusiasm, ate with gusto, giggled constantly, and was full of holiday cheer. He carried all his gifts around in a firmly clutched sack, afraid to let his newfound bounty out of his grasp. Jaclyn scolded her father for "hogging him"—Jaclyn was right about this. Laura said that when they told Lee that the schedule for the day involved visiting other family members first, he insisted that all he wanted was to see "Jiao Jiao"; he said good night to her photo each evening at bedtime and missed her almost as much as she missed him.

It was all I could do not to pinch myself to prove that it was finally real. I didn't care that my shambles of a house was decorated with green marker pigs. I didn't care if my tree fell down. I didn't care if the snow was a hassle. I didn't care if my cold continued for another three months. I didn't care how many guests descended on us. I didn't care how many nights I had to sleep in the Cinderella sleeping bag. I didn't even care that my toilet overflowed on Christmas day with a house full of guests. All I cared about was that we spent Christmas with Jaclyn's baby. And my heart rejoiced.

Chapter Twenty-six

A Time for Healing

The turning point in the process of growing up is when you discover
the core strength within you that survives all hurt.
—Max Lerner

I had long ago given up trying to change Jaclyn's mind about her life in China. I had valiantly tried to explain, to defend, to make her understand how and why her Chinese mother had given her up. She fiercely rejected my logic, mired in her own judgment about what had occurred. In the same manner, all her recollections about her life in the institution were of sorrow, of loss, of deprivation, and of need. Her baby and her friends were clearly the only glimmers of light in her past life.

Because I had come to know the determination in her spirit, I had slowly let go of the hope that anything would ever change on this score. I gave up any hope that she might one day want to return to Chinese school on Saturdays. I stopped trying to soften her memories and just listened to them. I stopped talking about all the things I loved about China to her so I did not have to listen to her fierce rebuttals. I assured her, when she told me on our last visit that she never wanted to return to China again, that she would never have to.

But in the same way that people seem to find true love when they finally stop searching for it, once I stopped hoping for something different, Jaclyn began to change.

She had heard us talking about our friends Al and Sandy, who were in the process of adopting from China. She surprised me by asking if she could go along with them on the trip.

"I'll ask Uncle Al if I can go, too, when he get his baby," she said to me.

"Why do you want to go, Jaclyn?" I asked, trying to mask my surprise.

"I want to visit Joan's house," she said. "Remember, she invite me." Joan had been our guide on our last trip, and Jaclyn adored her. So, true to her word, Jaclyn wrestled the phone from me the next time Uncle Al called.

"I go to China with you when you get you baby?" she asked. And always the advocate for those left behind, she assured Uncle Al, "There lot of good and pretty babies left in *my* China."

This surprise request was followed a few days later by a recollection: She talked of the fruit, like apples, that grew on trees in the orphanage compound. She remembered when they fell to the ground that her teacher would cut them into small pieces and give them to the children as treats. She loved them. She also remembered getting candy as treats on special occasions. She smiled as she recalled the kindness of the young teacher that I know she loved, in spite of her refusal to acknowledge it. The good memories were beginning to trickle through the cracks in the stone wall that she had built inside herself around her recall of that time.

A few days later, we were talking about her "China mama." We no longer had to do this under cover of darkness before she went to bed; the memory of her could now permeate the light. This time Jaclyn told me, "My China mama hug and kiss me."

Of course she did; I knew that all along. There was no way that a child could be as loving as Jaclyn without having known love herself. I thought now of how foolish I once was. Before I adopted, I envisioned these shadowy birth mothers as rivals for my child's love. Now I nearly cried with joy because my child realized, at some level, that her first mama loved her.

"She take care of me, but she not give me anything to eat. I hungry all the time," Jaclyn added. She still could not let go of this. The memory of that hunger was still too raw. In time, I hoped that she would be able to understand this, too.

I'm not sure what triggered the softening in her stance. Was it our last trip to China? Was it the fact that her baby was now home safely, and that the two children she truly loved, Lee and Jin Xun Li, were able to join her in the joy of this new life? Or was it simply the inevitable soothing that the passage of time brought with it? All I knew for sure was that the time for healing had begun.

Before I knew it, we were celebrating the one-year anniversary of Lee's adoption day. Because he had lived in my heart for what seemed an eternity, it was amazing to realize that he had only officially been in my

sister's family for a year. We all went to a Chinese restaurant to celebrate, and our combined offspring, both biological and adopted, loved
having a chance to dress in their traditional Chinese garb.

"I look like Chinese boy now!" Lee said, smiling at his reflection.

Lee is different from anyone else in my life in the sense that I never,
ever take him for granted. I can't keep my eyes off him whenever we are
together. I shamelessly beg him for hugs and kisses. I can't stop myself.
I know I shouldn't take anyone that I love for granted. But I have not yet
lost anyone whose place is in the inner sanctum of my heart. Those that
I love most, I see often. In the arrogant way of those who have not
known crushing grief, I assume that they will be there. But Lee is
exempted from that. Because I worried for so long about him, I never,
ever want to lose sight of him again.

On that night, as I reflected on the last year, I realized that the gift Lee
had brought with him was peace. He had brought peace to Jaclyn's
heart. I could bear to hear her prayers now. They had lost their frantic
edge, their jagged emotion, as she pleaded with God to bring her baby
home. And even though she never, ever laid her head down at night
without a prayer for Lee, these were now, finally, the prayers of a child.

Although still unusually small, Lee had blossomed in the past year
into a delightful, joy-filled sprite of a child. He bore no resemblance to
the emaciated, bug-bitten, balding waif we had met so long ago. He and
Jaclyn still delighted in each other. At her birthday party, Jaclyn saved
the seat next to her, the seat of honor, as she always did, for Lee. He
rejected the play clothes that his mother chose for him to wear to the
party. "I pick something else," he said firmly. He selected his good dress
pants, his white shirt and vest, and insisted on a tie and his "pretty
shoes."

"Now, Jiao Jiao say I handsome!" he said with a smile.

Lee would often talk about Jaclyn's caring for both him and the girl
named Po Po in the orphanage. Lee went through our photo albums
and pointed out Po Po for us. Jaclyn had always refused to do so. It was
as if she knew she could not save them all. She had to hold in her heart
only those that she loved most dearly.

Lee had shared some of his past and a few stories about the bullying that he endured after Jaclyn left the orphanage. Like Jaclyn's recollections, many were painful to hear. The most heart-wrenching was his account of a child kicking him in the back, many times, until he finally toppled onto the hard cement with such force that his nose was broken. This is what had caused the black-and-blue marks we had seen in one of the photos of him.

"Who do this to you?" Jaclyn asked him as she showed him the disturbing photo. He told the story and carefully pointed out the culprit while looking through our album.

"I knew it! I knew it was him! He very mean boy to Lee," Jaclyn said in a somber tone. "He not share his chair nicely with Lee at school. Lee never had enough chair. But I couldn't help him because he sat in the back and they made me sit in the front." And then later, with sadness, she asked, "Why God make mean boys?" But gone was her rage. He was safe. That was all that mattered to her now.

In a similar manner, Lee had brought peace to my heart, too. I, too, know that you can't save them all. While he lived there, his face, his pain, his sadness were all I could think about. Now the rest are faceless to me. Their hurt is less personal. I am not haunted in the same way by them. I still feel their need. But I don't know them the way I knew him. So the pain is now bearable.

But these kids have made me think of a bigger peace, too. Since the horror of September 11, 2001, like all of us I have been preoccupied with trying to fathom the hate in this world. I wonder how those who don't even know their enemy can be so filled with hate for them. And I think of all the children in this world who are victims of that hate.

It makes me reflect about how the United States first forged bonds with the people of China. I remember President Nixon's long-ago first trip to that mysterious country. Who would ever have thought that such different lands, lands that had closed each other out for so long, would be able to one day forge an alliance to help children? Could there be two more different cultures? Yet we've been able to put those differences aside and join together in a larger purpose—helping children find families.

I think, too, of my first trip to China to adopt my baby, Christy, and the close bonds we established with our guide there. She was a young woman in her twenties, and, as she got to know and trust us, she openly shared her thoughts about the international adoptions. She confided that many of her contemporaries thought she was wrong to work in the adoption program. She said that they felt humiliated by having "rich Americans" come and "buy their babies." They would say, scoffing, "They take advantage of China because it is a poor country. But once we have money, we will go there and buy their babies." I asked our guide how she responded.

"I tell them to go to the places I have gone and see what I have seen. I invite them to see the orphanages for themselves and then tell me that this is wrong." And with a smile she added, "I tell them how much you love the children."

But then she shared this heartache, too. She told me about one of the first families she had helped to adopt and how they had recently returned with their now five-year-old daughter. "But 'Ni hao' was all she could say in Chinese," she said with obvious sadness. "Li Dan is a Chinese girl. Promise me you will teach her about her proud homeland. Promise me that when she visits, she will know Chinese." I solemnly promised. Li Dan, now my Christy, is four years old. In spite of my good intentions, "Ni hao" is all she can say in Chinese.

And I ask myself, too, how I would feel if Chinese citizens came here and adopted American babies. Would I be able to trust them to teach those children how great our country is? Would I be able to smile and say "lucky baby" while flashing a thumbs-up sign the way they do? Would I be as gracious and as welcoming as they are, putting the needs of the child first?

I think, too, of our trip to Jaclyn, taken just three weeks after the United States had accidentally bombed a Chinese embassy in Africa. There was a travel advisory in place, and I had watched the anti-U.S. demonstrations on TV with some apprehension. The topic surfaced during one meeting that we had with Chinese officials, and I was quick to offer an apology. I'll never forget what happened next. The official looked directly into my eyes and said, "Government is government," with a dismissive air. Then she took my hand and said, "But people are people."

It's a distinction I think of often. We're all so much more the same than we are different. I'm grateful for the way the Chinese have never allowed political matters to affect the adoption program. These children are ultimately the bridge between our two very different countries. They are, like Lee, the peacemakers.

Whenever I despair about the hate in this world, I only have to look at my mail to see another truth. Nearly every week I get an email from an unknown friend who asks for an update on how Lee is doing. Jaclyn receives birthday cards from loving people that we have never met. And I know how many special little ones live in my heart, too. Children whose stories I have followed. Children I have prayed for, yet never met. There is more goodness, more love, more caring in this world than there is hate. I know it. I feel it. As long as we continue to reach out to each other through these kids, we will continue to forge a path toward peace.

Lee always said in his recounting of his experiences that he never, ever struck another child. Lee, like Jaclyn, cannot stand to see the suffering of others. He is the first on the scene if any of his sisters starts to cry. He dissolves into their grief. He comforts, too. He cannot bear to see them punished. I had worried that the bullying, the hate-filled moments, the hurts in the institution would have stolen from him the capacity to empathize and care. But this child knows how to love. He has been wronged, but he knows how to forgive; he knows how to offer comfort. How, then, can we offer less?

So I've learned some powerful lessons about forgiveness in the last year. But that isn't all. What else has Jaclyn brought into my life?

Exhaustion. My weariness amazed me. But she gave me energy, too. Her delightful sense of humor. Her sparkle. The way her countenance was illuminated from within. She was not a spectator in life but was really, truly alive and went full throttle ahead into everything. And her vitality pushed me to help others, too. Without her prodding, I would be so much less. She expected so much that she made me be my best self. Thanks, Jaclyn.

Noise. Jaclyn brought a level of din into my previously quiet life and household that I was still getting used to. Her voice, her shouts, her cries could not be ignored. And she nagged at my soul like no other; *tenacious* did not even begin to describe it.

And the result? Even a U.S. senator heard her voice and vowed to help bring her baby here. I was in awe of her need to be heard. A noisy household was a small price to pay for this new voice in my life. Thanks for opening my ears, Jaclyn.

Truth. Her simple truths altered forever the way I saw the world. It was not a safe place for children. Children suffered in ways that made no sense, that had no rhyme or reason or cause except their circumstances of birth. Children everywhere were denied basic needs and, as a result, any chance to have a childhood. But she had shown me this truth, too: in the darkest of circumstances, love can not only survive but thrive, as evidenced by Jaclyn's love for her baby. And this truth: for every person who walked by and refused to acknowledge suffering as part of their responsibility, there were countless others desperate to open their hearts and lives and homes to make these children their own. How lucky I felt to know so many of these everyday heroes.

And what else had knowing Jaclyn taught me?

That love could heal, but not overnight. Healing takes time. Trust takes time. Love takes time. And sometimes even love is not enough. Children who are hurt have an empty place in their souls that can seem bottomless, and my best efforts, my deepest love, cannot begin to fill this cavernous space.

That people were not always what they seemed. Jaclyn's quest to bring her baby home had shown me that some flesh-and-blood people were secretly heroes and angels. And that powerful changes could start with tiny people.

That I could fall in love again. But this time with the tiniest, scrawniest, most pathetic little guy on the playground, Xiao Mei Mei. How grateful I was to hold him in my arms again.

That my ability to sleep at night had nothing to do with money in the bank, a good job, or a strong marriage. It had everything to do with knowing that the child I loved slept under my roof, safe at last. How well I finally rest now that Xiao Mei Mei is home.

That dreams could come true. Children that seemed out of our grasp, too deeply mired in government rules and paperwork, too stuck in the system, could mysteriously, miraculously become our own. That the impossible was possible with God in your corner and His connections on your side.

That when I looked at life through the eyes of a hurt child, everything was different. But how privileged I felt to have this vision—not that it wasn't excruciatingly painful to experience, but it changed everything. My new vision forced me to focus my life differently. And, in doing so, I found that suddenly my life had even greater meaning and richness.

Thanks, Jaclyn. Thanks for turning my life upside down. Thanks for being patient with me. Thanks for finding it in your soul to trust me. Thanks for letting me be your mom. Thanks for taking my hand.

Afterword

L ee continues to thrive in his new life. Amazingly, he hasn't had any adjustment issues. He attends kindergarten now but shared Jaclyn's lack of enthusiasm for Chinese school. Lee is a spirited, loving little boy who embraces life. Jaclyn's sureness that he was a truly special little soul could not have been more on target. His sister Willow has blossomed into a shy, sweet, loving little girl that captivates everyone she meets. She is also startlingly beautiful. Lee and Willow are shining examples of the resilience of the human spirit. They embrace life; love is healing them.

True to the spirit of adoption, where each child seems to bring another here, Jeff's brother and his wife recently returned from China with a delightful new son who shares Jaclyn's birthday. Lee now has Chinese siblings and cousins on both sides of the family and a Chinese boy cousin to boot. As the adoption of boys from China is still a rarity, this was an unexpected blessing.

Jaclyn is now seven years old. She has so completely assimilated into her new life that she is in many ways undistinguishable in a group of children. In some ways, she is an extraordinary child. But what she is most of all is an ordinary child who has just seen too much of this world.

Lee and Jaclyn have a bond unlike any I have ever seen. Jaclyn still smothers him with love every time she sees him and laughs at his attempts to wipe her kisses off. At the end of any fun-filled holiday, Laura always asks Lee what his favorite part of the day was. "See Jiao Jiao" is his standard reply. Jaclyn has hidden among her secret treasures a letter that he sent her along with a beautifully painted butterfly. He dictated these words to his mother:

Dear Jiao Jiao,
I love you. You're my best friend. I made my butterfly at my

*school. You're my best friend in the whole world. Thank you for tak-
ing care of me in China.*
    Love,
    Lee.

As this book goes to print, we are all anxiously awaiting word about
Jeff's job transfer to Kentucky. At first I was devastated by the thought
of them moving; I couldn't even imagine how I would explain it to
Jaclyn. I think she will be able to stand it because she knows that Lee is
safe and loved. I've come to realize that these children have a bond that
even a five-hour distance will not alter. The love between them will
never change.

Another thing that does not change is Jaclyn's prayers for Lee. To this
day, he continues to be first in her thoughts and prayers each night. She
still remembers to thank God for bringing her baby here. Even now,
after all this time, I can't write those words without tears.

Jaclyn told me recently that she had decided what she wanted to be
when she grew up. I had been ready to send her name to the American
Civil Liberties Union. Given her keen sense of justice and her desperate
need to advocate for the helpless, I figured they could recruit her early.
But, as in all things, she had her own ideas: "When I grow up I want to
be just like Snow White. I want to go to China and bring the babies here
and find them mamas." I nodded, and she continued, "But I want you
go with me and help me, Mama."

Ironically, I had been preparing to do just that. After much inner tur-
moil, I quit my job as a school administrator and have decided to make
adoption my life's work. I'd been worried about the effect of this decision on my family's finances. But Jaclyn set me straight. "Babies more
'portant than money," she told me. Indeed.

If you have come to love Jaclyn, please note that I am working on a
second book about her adjustment to America. This one will be filled
with mostly humorous anecdotes. Its working title is *You Don't Say
Stinky in Church . . . and Other Life Lessons Learned from Jaclyn.*

My mom always says that true love, real love, lasting love is forged by
the stuff you have been through together. So, given what we've been

through together, I guess it's no surprise that Jaclyn and I have a bond unlike any that I have ever experienced with another. I love her fiercely. And she is equally devoted to me.

Jaclyn continues to be the joy of my life and also the greatest challenge in it. I can't deny that adopting Jaclyn was, without a doubt, the hardest thing I've ever done. But adopting Jaclyn was also, without a doubt, the best thing I've ever done. I guess that saying is true: nothing in life worth doing is easy. Because I've been so candid about how hard that first year was, how ill-prepared and afraid I was, how sure I was that this child's needs were beyond my parenting abilities, those considering an older child adoption often ask me, "If you had known then what you know now, would you still have done it?"

The answer to that one is easy: in a nanosecond.

List of Photographs